1985

Geoffrey Grigson

COLLECTED POEMS
1963–1980

Allison & Busby
LONDON / NEW YORK

First published 1982 by
Allison and Busby Limited,
6a Noel Street, London W1V 3RB, England
and distributed in the USA by
Schocken Books Inc.,
200 Madison Avenue, New York, NY 10016

British Library Cataloguing in Publication Data

Grigson, Geoffrey
  Collected poems 1963–1980
  I. Title
  821′.912   PR6013.R744

  ISBN 0-85031-419-4

Typeset by Alan Sutton Publishers Limited, Gloucester
and printed in Great Britain by
The Camelot Press, Southampton.

Contents

3. POEMS 1975–1980

11

Poems 1963–1969

Heart Burial

They fetched it along, and they slipped it in,
Mr Hardy's heart in a biscuit tin.

Mrs Hardy said, This grave is my bed
And my husband Thomas was not well-bred.

And the heart spoke up, and it mildly said,
Give me to my old dog Wessex instead,

Give me to my surly dog Wessex instead,
But Wessex was busy with a fresh sheep's head,

And the rector pretended he did not hear,
And dry was the sexton and needed beer,

And bumpetty bump and din din din
Earth fell on the box and the biscuit tin.

Basic Substances

Mineral grains that I contain perhaps
were once in some abysmal tory dunce,
or in a salted head or taut remains
that dunce had hung in windy chains,

or save the mark they might have been
once sainted, scented grains
processed and censed in ganging games.
Each cat extends into his close-

furred flea, and my environment's
contained in me. Same substances compound
us two. That's clear, dear love,
and true, whatever you or I may do.

15

Night Stroll

My emanations of the ultra-mean are multiple,
Grey-skinned, not often heard or seen. Yet walking
Down—when shops are shut—an empty half-lit street
Occasionally I hear them caterwaul, on heat,

Then pad up alleys on their hard-skinned feet. They go
To ground: there comes the faintest clatter of a dust-
Bin lid. Occasionally I face one, though
I'd rather not, flattened behind a downpipe

On the wall. I aim a blow with book or walking-stick,
Hit nothing but the dull stock brick.
Then winter darkens, and I see
A vague shape hunched on dirty snow,

I hear a hissing, smell a ferret-steam of one
Such creature nonchalantly pissing. Ghosts
Of living, I reflect, not dead. And crawl moodily on
With cold thighs to my double bed.

Our Mr Molar

New certainties, they say, which overcrowd the mental tum,
New highly likely but unwelcome sociological notions
Induce distention, cause dry wind, and
Knobbly, rather irregular and difficult motions.

Take our Mr Molar, chairman of our local
Conservative and Unionist, or White Man's party,
J.P. and vicar's warden, and now twenty stone.
I knew him as a fourteen stone front-row rugger hearty

And see him on Friday evenings meeting
His neither hearty nor nice-looking offspring at our station
Togged in white shorts, short socks, and sweater, and looking
Sour about the state—under the socialists—of our deluded
   nation.

16

God bless me, won't someone touch a cap to him?
Show the respect that's due to dough not earned but
    tidily invested?
But the truth of the matter is that no one now
Wears that style of cap, grows forelocks, or is interested.

And the truth of the matter further is, it's not state of the
    nation,
Socialism or such crap that graves his sheep's brow with
    that noble frown.
It's too much eating, fears of years, not getting onions
And regretting them—he's like the rest of us—that gets
    old Molar down.

Lecture Note: Elizabethan Period

He wrote a final poem down. Then died
Before the liquid shining on the three last letters dried.
It fluttered from his table to the floor
Where kittens played with it while daughters cried.
For days it lay in fluff and dust behind the door.
A maid then picked it up, to have the solar
Tidy for the funeral bakes, and dropped it in the jakes.
So fate had him and all the rest of us well bitten.
Now irretrievably beshitten, it was, dear sirs,
The one immortal poem he had written.

Coincidence of 10 p.m.

A scent of quinces and a lunar bow—
A donnée, so the smart reviewers say—.
What should be done with it I do not know,
A scent of quinces and a lunar bow.

                                        Saint-Jacques

On a Change of Style

Peers have been made whose hired robes have hidden
A depth of wallowing in the dirtiest midden.
Here was a lord—his hopes and head were both too big—
Who doffed his ermine and revealed a pig.

On Certain Motions Tranquilly Recollected

Marvell's poem on Caesarean section came to them when
   they recalled
A day on Moth Ledge in the Isles. But this was making
   love, or child;
Not birth. Their act was warm, yet comic somewhat on a
   wet
Weed bed: Not violent, like Marvell's birth, though wild.

She tied, Love's banneret, salt pants to a walking-stick,
Then held them in a brisk wind till they dried.
The tide returned, and hid Moth Ledge, where so to say
They had made a sub-Atlantic child.

To a Poet's Biographer

Find out what boy he was, how
His unrecognized needs were fed,
What rocks his brilliant redstarts flickered from,
Feel for the slag or bilberry bank that held his head.

Enter his blue Eden by this grace. Then
His young and later Hell. Remembering
You do not grind a felling axe in your
Green limestone dell; and that you wish him well.

Louis MacNeice
September 2nd, 1963

I turned on the transistor:
By luck, for your sorrel,
Your *Vol de Nuit,*
It was Haydn,

Black and diffident man
Of the bog and the stoa
Whose rush of love
Was rejected,

Whose wolfhound
Bent round my table,
Who are no longer around
In your Chinese

Garden of poems.
Where one is of water,
On which tea-yellow
Leaves of another

Are falling, always
Are falling, this one
Is a stone by itself,
On which you inscribe

With invisible legible letters
That unrest of the soul
Which you found
So wryly appalling.

You have gone: will
No longer arrange
In sunlight with wit
Your aloneness.

But, classical quizzical
One, whose scent is
Sharp in the centre,
Your garden is open.

Saddish Day in Spring

Picking again, having driven miles,
Marsh marigolds from cracking sticks, decayed
Bog stems, grey-soaked leaves, wet black, all

Previous years. A ritual, some weeks always
Before coarse Honesty flares on garden mounds.
On mounds: Marlborough, they said, meant Merlin's

Mound: it means, precisely, Mound of Marigolds,
Most glazing pigment in our natural box.
Yet either way a glitter. It is the youngest

Only of our party cares. Wind blows chimney smoke
Downhill: it is this stinging wind
Creates our tears, the situation neither

Saccharine nor bitter. The ritual's
Carried through, one branch bent back, another
Snapped, an unsqueegeeing foothold found, knobs

Still green selected—tears in our eyes, drops
Swinging from our reddest noses both
Devoid of meaning, no feelings in us resurrected.

A New Tree

It is April, she is held
to the window
to see leaves of our new
weeping willow, less

green than a yellow:
I love what she is; and
may be—that she gives,
and is given, so lives

now, and again
in a heaven,
there will be heavy
absence of light

and cold rain,
but I love
in her that at times
the quick drops

should catch light
down the pane, a sun
being fiercely
let loose again.

Brightness Falls from the Air

The coachload have been to the sea.
Their coach starred yellow with lights
In a row, creeps down in a half-dark, ob-
Servable small from a distance,

The sideways steep of a hill.
Carries children, women who bore them.
Men. They are singing. Sex jokes are
Ancient as Bruegel. Hands feel,

Why not, over knees. Some are drunk,
Are wearing small hats. Have bought
Other mementoes. Their coach
Made of many inventions,

Illusions, turns
Obeying the road at a hairpin,
Further descends into thickening
Of dark, towards home.

Several Colours

Green.
A mineral green should be preferred,
Or chemical. In vitrifactions, or
Stuffed plumage of a bird.
I do not myself despise
A sharp green in skies.

Red.
In prayerbooks, sentimental.
Excellent, but rare, in wax.
Otherwise about red,
Hammers, sickles, cardinals, altogether
Too much is said.

Blue.
I am against it in skies
Or in conceitedly quivering eyes. For it,
In rounded pieces of pitted glass
On beaches among wrecks and wracks,
And I must confess in flax.

Black.
Well, there are various blacks.
Indubitably the best are
Worn by white.
Otherwise I don't much
Go for the night.

White—
As above, if not absolute or too
Unrelievedly white. But it's not
My religion: it invites
Dirt,
Does white.

Leaving yellow,
Which is no good bedfellow.
Outside—well, let it be lemon.
Inside under dishes dyed
Into uneven linen. It doesn't otherwise
Much go with women.

A Skull in Salop

The needs of nature lead to common
postures in strange places: above,
the Norman motte, the moat below,
and old chrysanthemums from graves.

The church behind me, yew
beside me, and my left hand
finds, the felt clean shape at first
unrecognized, a pate.

I rise relieved, though that's
not quite the word; and stand; and see
azured extents below again,
feeling the cool of air.

Richard's Castle

Looking for things which were fun,
  Hanging round on the way,
When I was young they complained
  I was late, again day after day.

When they caught me they beat me,
  Late again, Grigson III, they would say.
But the boot has changed feet and I see
  It grows late in the day.

You'll never learn, they insisted,
  Be late for your funeral, they'd say.
Late again for parade, and for prep, and for prayers,
  I admit, now it's late in the day,

I was always behind, but I ask them
  If they can honestly say
Their breakfast of worm was so good
  For them, day after day.

Lovers Who Meet in Churches
(Mary Godwin's letter to Shelley,
October 25th, 1814)

Lovers who meet in churches
And sit there indifferent to God,
Or dead. Priests, this is a charity
You most unwillingly provide,
This privacy. You cannot hear
Her pagan heart by the chill
Tomb-chest pounding. Her words,
O my own one be happy,
O my love, my dear.

Your Way

A green lorry piled to a risky sway
Of brown cubes of hay lurches
My way, under the grey of one more
Nearly wet, late summer day.

But you are young.
I have turned the car
And I drive your way.

Semence des Premiers Dieux
*The flowers they picked—or
so they hoped—were death.*

Observe: a failing moon theatrically was poised:
night went: around the yellowing slip
came blue and brown.

Slight as their fingers, bent white
glistening tubes they picked, these
naked two, wading to thighs

Through burrs. One straightened,
watched the thin moon strike down,
held her flowers' ice against her,

Paused and plucked off burrs. Business
of the semi-dark was done. Quickly
venomous flowers lose venom in the sun.

The Hunt

The wax-red roofings of the dawn
Suffuse with pink a milky Unicorn
Who steps through May-wet flowers and eyes
The crawling hunters with a faint surprise.

They set their spears around:
He clears their avaricious circle at a bound,
He neighs, he shakes a blood-tipped horn,
This wounded, pure, contemptuous Unicorn.

Then stops. Then snuffs a different scent.
And now his delicate knees are bent,
And though he understands the trap,
He lays his snowy beard along the Virgin's lap.

Piss-piped Cities of the Plain

*"The high quality of the sanitary arrangements at
Mohenjo-daro could well be envied in many parts of the
world today. . . The whole city bespeaks middle-class
prosperity with zealous municipal control."*

Indra, fort-cracker, stamped over the river.
Men were felled in their cities' uppermost alleys.
Stank there, unburied. Then dried.
In brick docks at Lothal on the Gulf
Boats rotted. Rotted boats gently sank with their cargo.
All things had ended. Those who survived
For a while, ill and decrepit, did not foresee
Indra's also piss-piped, let's say, Chicago,

Where in a museum paid for by the final
Squealing of pigs they imitate nature's
Minutest venation; where an institute
Hogs pictures from Peking and Paris, Siena and Venice,
And knows how they made them; where a grey Indus
From anus and bladder and balls
Rolls ever away and away.

Wild Doves Arriving

There is a contrast between the high flight of doves
And their douce behaviour two by two in hedges.
They fly in parties. Their wings are sharp and quick and nervy.
They have purpose. Their quick flight pauses, doves drop away
In ones for now new green of hedges, where flight from
   branch
To branch inside is nothing wild. Mated, their ringed
Eyes, their melody, are mild. "Dove-grey," we say,
   "dove-grey."
At times they walk for smoothness on quiet roads.
A car approaches. Spreading white tails they rise
And are once more invisibly absorbed in hedges.

Oxford Philosophers

Backsides of philosophers bitten by the rain,
Colour of stale wet grass in winter,
Most surprised I should be, Ancient Wisdoms,
To walk down to the pavement and find
Your blank eyeballs cut sharp again.

No one restores you, Old Clichés; will remain
Prognathous, a row of no ones. Though no one knows
Which of you is which, I think you may be
Those who have found out, and pettishly a bit have
   petrified
Deliberately your senses, making it plain

By your eroding sneers that shall I say Ayer or Alain
Or Daily Mail astrologers are all or
Much the same. Sparrows shit on your rude
Knobs, psephologists, symbol on symbol
Till the next sideways sluice of rain.

It does seem you win the game.
Even if tamped under lumps of the fake
Temples round you, idiot archaeologists with echo
Apparatus will detect you, again crane you to your
Iron-stained stone sneers against the rain.

Lovers in a Train

Quickly arrive and go the suavest
ploughlands of most ancient age. These
I reflect on, ploughed

Before Brittonic speakers came; which
she, there, does not know; and if she did,
quite right, she would not care.

Her eyebrows black, her fair falling hair
from her sloped head on his
green cardigan, her legs

Are long, visible to above
her knees, having a full fineness of her
being young. Under the dusk nylons

Finest hair. Headlines of politics, rats' run,
say I in silence, face her and quite right
she is, she does not care.

He is blue-chinned, a hairy man, for her wild man
all of her sinuous care: he would have been
a short-browed hard black-thatched thin-

Waisted Roman charioteer; sees through sloped
slits of black not chi-rho monograms, but
her. His most knobbed bone-wristed hands

In a relaxed cat's entwinement held by her
so delicate ones. Tresses—I pick that antique
winding word—fairly across her blackest

Eyebrows sway, her sweet head nested under
now her tender savage's unlobed and stark
most startlingly red-tinted ear.

Hollowed Stone

Looked for the Hollowed Stone
On a wrong height on the down.
Considered death, considered dying alone.
Discovered no sign of the stone.

Encountered a bull where I expected the stone,
Grazing head down; raised a bull-eye
As if I were a stone. With heifers.
By no means alone.

In the last light discovered the stone,
In a wired copse under the down.
Nettly, much overgrown. Was stung,
Regarded this work. Continued alone.

In a House, a Beginner

I say, Upper Middle?
and do you reject, I further enquire,
the large house you grew in,
two nurseries,
one drive and
three gardens, also

one wide waterfall? You
do not at all,
they were given, and you
accept all, china, or
chinese-white, china-
clay mounds

on the blue
extreme of your seeing
past very small
fuchsia skirts swinging,
wigs on a wall,
purple port

on a heart-
rotten family tree
you repeat coolly "when
senses were sharpest
were given, beginning
a freedom in me."

March 1st, 1964

No Metaphysic

Project this light, make
gilded wires of rain, O eight-
wheeled truck invisible!

Leave in to-night a humming
after-note, O bell
not now being swung!

My God, I trust that's plain—
what your extinctness sparks
soon is extinct again.

Re-tolling a Dry Word

Woke before sunlight, after a dream of you, walked
To the half-hatch door, inspected the night,
Heard a crowing, bricks chill to my feet. I had looked

From a high window, I mean in my dream, down, down
To a pavement across a wide street. It was too far
To see how you looked or for hearing you speak.

But by your slightness and walk I knew each time
It was you, and when my dream broke I re-tolled
A small bell with the dry word "remote."

Always you went with a man I never knew, not the man
I suppose you are still married to. Something to see you
After these years, now ten, without change: not

To regret, or complain or feel pain. Cavafy has taught me
That much, to recall, to be glad. To think
Of delight, drinking rosé again, thinking back,

Though you might be dead, to the look
Of our room and the way
That you kicked the light clothes off the bed.

Not Visited Enough

Not visited enough, each poet knows
His deadly fondness for his own mishaps,
The way he fails to sort the full-term births
From all his misengendered scraps.

After a Death

Dead men thought this landscape theirs,
I think, or hesitate to think it mine,
Having my fears. Dead men heard orioles

Pronounce themselves inside the twist
Of trees, those invisible birds who reach
This north, and find no cherries red:

Rougiront, loriot, oriole: dead
Men loved, but also had their fears.
Oriole, loriot, rougiront touched

Tenderly their ears. Loved,
And were loved. Some prayed. Few
Could beat back their fears.

Trôo

31

After Reading an Autobiography

Louis, across the intervening sagging years
A straighter line of sight recalls
Your black-mopped boy condemned to bleaker
Childhood than your own, your white-faced

Stiff silent sister fetching him. The Dresden
Sherpherdess had left. Betsy your hound
Bent in right angles round my furniture,
Was elegant and tall, and smelt. I lacked

Both nerve and words to show I recognized
Your eyes were on the Roman general, Time,
Mounted below the brutish arch, fearing
Upon the cast-iron fancy stepway

To the foxglove garden those first friends
Of yours, mincing and epicene, as you,
Most black-avised, were not; and as you turned
Fragments of opal in the tube of oil

Sometimes I saw your uncut nails were black.
From you pissed up at chosen times in decent
Isolation, poems on half-sheets came, each word
Exact in angled ink, sharp runes of power

Which you had cut, late voyager to the sacred city,
On the grey northern tomb or warmed white
Marble of the lion's haunch. "This day,
Interpret it in your own way, Christ was born."

Death in his deep pothole caught you, a long
While having stalked you. Your quest was ended,
No dark tower entered, or defended, no fake
Solution proffered to us all. And now

Crossing the downs upon the decent chalk
I see you in white shorts cycling, in bright
Winds of March; walking aloof, bike lent against my
Sarsen stones, mortal and young.

Partial Account

Tomb has given us about his Muse
More than once misleading news:
It isn't that she acts by whim,
Tomb bullies others, so she bullies him.

Two Presidents and Three Widows

Captain, O Captain, when the other one died
A man in the passage cried Come inside.
Inside there was clinking, laughing, drinking,
Shouting, bouncing about on the bed,
And here's what the man in the doorway said,
Have a drink with us, fellow, the cripple is dead.

Captain, O Captain, you're holed in the head

And the things which are thought are not openly said.
There may not be clinking, laughing, drinking,
Shouting, bouncing about on the bed
And three widows are weeping, and another one's dead.

Poets in Generations

Journalist–dons, hair–oiled ad–men,
mountaineers with such scabbed

asses' ears, you make us level layers
laid down in your sleazy sea.

Not countering crap with crap,
I shan't repudiate your soft

geology by claiming *magma, welling up,*
intruding, cooling, columnar,

33

broken short, may be. At any rate
we're not the shale that drips

such oil upon your hair. We claim
at least an unconformity.

Marginal Observation on a Tennysonian Theme

It is to-day always: to-day huge trees
Under a housing of grey shed bitter
Light they absorbed: ribbed short
Flames of leaves crowd drily the roots of these
Dumb trees to-day. Shift over ankles.
Banked brilliant, scented with
Needed dying is to-day.

On a Dry Hill

On a dry hill, with skulls,
—Or so they say, a nailed man screamed;
At which moment of which hour
On which initial day,
So intense was their dismay, locked
Atoms shattered into flower.

That's what they say. Flashes
Zipped the black air in three. They say
Thin-lipped and blind could see
In a wild wind a nailed and naked dead man
On a tree.

The show's forbidden on TV.

On Reading Again the Poetry of Clere Parsons

We are not collected poems yet, my dear—
how dangerous to say because how soon you were:
young, thin, tall, white face under pale hair,

you enter T.S. Eliot's room, and I see still
as you lean forward in your walk, your lips'
curling curious authority as if isolated in the air.

Now bent with another over glistening modish bows,
the peak of Teide floating in the air,
I watch fish fly, or slide, bright, from sudden whiteness

and re-enter blue. Clere,
your poems hint and glint. I think
death made them break the sea. That rootless

restful peak Donne pondered on, stays high. Again,
   again,
again, out of white, back into blue, winged bright
fish which are real, most briefly, suddenly fly.

Objects
"Moments of vision are blurred rapidly, and the
poet sinks into the rhetoric of the will." — Wyndham Lewis

On a sill:
Black and white stripes,
A pink scarf, amethyst edge of a
Flannel, ballet shoes red,
Blue stockinged blunt
Feet of a bear, head
To a vaguely wood-
Coloured brick: I am surprised
Noticing suddenly
These, waiting there.

A starling nicks with its bill,
Sky is quite grey. Inside
I notice no fumble or blunder
Or fuss of the will.
No connection. I notice only
Extravagant wonder
Of items laid out on a long
White painted sill.

Encouragement, on a Leaf

Written on a gold leaf in Greek
    Take Courage—
and we who survived placed the leaf
under your hands, so that without
all loss of hope you might meet indifferent
Charon, and cross the cold Styx.

Friend, things have changed. Charon we meet,
the cold river flows through our lives. If,
as we shut you away, if
you could pass out to ourselves in your grey
claw from your peace
the gold leaf on which
Take Courage is written.

Baroque Wedding

Saints, white pigeons perched on cornices,
Outburst of music over the western door.
Pink putti raise their arms,
Ancients with blown beards scan folios, straight
Gilded rays compete.

Now peasants for a wedding step
Into this interrupted icing and this gold. Gilded

Smooth pillars slide
Above this stubby girl and work-shaped man
Who rise. Music repeats its roar.
A flash-bulb goes. Mostly holy skeletons
In coloured net wait under altars
Of this white and gold.

Banz

"Where Sproutlands Flourish"

"Where sproutlands flourish" — not a place for me.
I much dislike the hard stems coming back, prefer
to rip them clear, even if they
include Sweet Bay, I clean the corner and the bricks,
I add a roof of sorts,
and make a ruin serve.

    And when this corner dries, persistently I sweep
out ants, dust, sowpigs and leaves, setting
a pure white table there (rustless
I mean), some liquor, flowers arranged, plus
a transistor, for the news.

H.C. for the Supine

Anyone for Holy Communion was said
by a voice past our bay which still in the
distance cheerily trilled *What! no one today!*

It was a priest C. of E. sailed
with knees up, if you see what I mean, past
our bay: he well could have changed his

spanking along for a more sensible pace, I would say,
but he had us all on our backs in each bay
to be slipped if need be to his vague Future Day,

37

in all of which there's a moral, as Alfie the atheist
driver, dry man of our bay with tubes through his
mouth and his nose, if he could, weakly would say.

Her Leftish Life a Little, Shall We Say, Too North West Three

Was lived along an edge of years,
   A most uncomfortable edge,
Not in the blue field of flowers at
   First, but in its sharp-wired hedge.

Then never among private lawns
   Between candid shrubs of May
Nor even in the public parks
   Yawning the other way,

But always up between the two
   On a most narrow wall
Nervous along the top with glass,
   From which she dared not fall.

Red Ribbon, Marseillaise, and Oradour

*"Rusted fire-twisted sewing-machines, picked out of the
ruins, rest on the window-sills of each house at Oradour,
adding an extra poignancy to this most poignant scene of
Nazi massacre."* — Guidebook

It was French Armistice Day before midday, it was
freshly in May, school-children in flower with the
flowers in their hands processed to the square where by
Monsieur le Maire was made chevalier

A black-trousered ex-sergeant short in one leg pinned
at last to a cross and a ribbon of red. Tri-
colours flew and nobody knew there was any-
thing wrong with that bloodthirsty song they

Sang to blue air. As their voices spattered
mildly that square I thought how in windows
of houses burnt out, in silence I'd seen a morning
before the red sewing-machines of mad Oradour.

The Old False Leg

Three crows hopped on an old false leg,
    On an old false leg,
    An old false leg,
Three crows hopped on an old false leg
    Which lay out alone on the moor.

Whoever could have dropped that old false leg,
    Old false leg,
    That old false leg,
Whoever could have dropped that old false leg,
    Out by the lake on the moor?

It was nobody dropped that old false leg,
    Old false leg,
    Old false leg,
It was nobody dropped that very false leg,
    Which slept out alone on the moor.

That old false leg jumped up on its toes,
    Up on its toes,
    Up on its toes,
That old false leg jumped up on its toes,
    In the very wet mist on the moor,

And it hit the tail feathers off those crows,
    Off those crows,
    Off those crows,
And it hit the tail feathers off those crows,
    Caw, caw, caw on the moor.

And those crows flew away quite nakedly,
  Quite nakedly,
  Quite nakedly,
And those crows flew away quite nakedly,
  Into the mist on the moor.

And the false leg thereupon strolled to the shore,
  Strolled to the shore,
  Strolled to the shore,
And the false leg thereupon strolled to the shore,
  Into the lake, and was seen no more,
  Seen no more

A Painter of Our Day

He teaches me what is: never nostalgia,
Yet never contempt for what has been composed.
With "strangle the swan" I sympathize:
He would not paint a swan or a rose.
I would not write them. He says don't disregard
The single swan drawing a glittering circumflex
Along your river avenue: look — *Allons*
Voir si la rose? — No, but into
Its packed centre. Recognizing there much
Old reiterated wisdom of perceiving?
No, seeing what you see: what is.

  At Verneuil, round Thérèse of Lisieux
After her first communion (but "she" is
A whiteness in the light and shadow)
Maurice Denis has woven roses (but they
Are shape, in a selection of the curves
That roses in a small back garden here
Are made to take, among the shadows
And the lights). M. le Curé says —
The dull historian of ideas, dull

Courtauld lecturer says — seldom what is,
Which is for each of us. I do not say transfer,
Translate, transplant, transpose, only accept the old
Swan of snow; again, the rose whose pink contains
A blue, if either comes my way.

   This my old friend teaches me. I say, I see
This, that, in your abstract pictures, he says
Not quite no. I say, This blue space is that small
Window in your studio or is Atlantic Penwith
Blue, through a dolmen. Slightly he shrugs away.

I say, The title says. He says, I find the titles
Afterwards. Titles are difficult: suggest a title
For this picture here. Children need names,
I must reflect, and I am taught again to accept
What is; also, that always each wonderful realm
He makes and the immense realm each other penetrate.

   Yet of the few painters, or few poets, each
Of us can live by, most have been
Long dead: they are Collected Works,
Their Retrospective, their Memorial
Exhibition all the time is here.
The centre of them, where they most exist, in
Freedom, has to accept each friend, each devotee.
Suddenly when young or in our first ability
We find them, slowly we find the reasons
For our love, finding ourselves, and what we lack
As well or need the most. It is about this,
This centre, historians of art or poetry
Cook their most tedious fudge, missing
Or smearing each realm-maker's liberty; it is the real,
Like you, who win, against art's pedants,
Art's officials, and art's auctioneers: innocent
You say your first Cumbrian landscapes were
As my small girl, who swopped her puns with you,
Seeing them again — "after 50 (500) years"
You write — in Bâle. I saw innocent
Pictures by you first; and you once showed
Me, reproduced, Raphael's Three Graces, not to say

Pink and pure white spiralling pencils that
I find again each June in striped petunias.

   Last year you threw a ball, loving its line of
Sheer, rebounding curves, in light,
You spoke in the long room floating

Above the lake of Raphael, Giorgione, Tobey,
Braque, Cézanne, of blue, and of discovery, and
Of the power of lasting like Cézanne, in art,
To the extreme end: with age combining
Unimaginable Giorgione's youth I watched you,
Watched your pictures (in which stronger innocence
For the organized above all accidents survives),
Heard you, in your centre again, saddened
By leaving you and by your physical age,
And by the snow and sleet after your sunshine
Round the Alpine train.
                  Then days, days after
Were irradiated round me by your truth.

Trôo

Archaeological Note

When horizontal light unites the rim
and scollop of their plateau, one specially
sees, by smoothness, how it was their

Comfort's hollow, whatever call for blood
came with a greedy mother god. Hills
lay back and curved. Their flocks ahead,

This was air's commonwealth, this
raised hollow. Under, round all,
marshes, sweaty madness, blackthorns, trees,

Man-eating elves, uncertainty's kingdom
in whose most netted thicket, the teller
of necessary tales declared in evening

Bivouacs by the smooth bowl-barrows
of the dead, elves guarded with long
teeth and care a scented powerful

Flower, a white flower, by juice of which
might pocks be smoothed, members up-ended,
sagged breasts delightfully again distended.

Bishops Cannings

Toussaint

Bitter holiday. A wedge briefly of eastern orange splits
our unfeatured earth from a less featured sky: red on a
  white wall
spreads, wavers, in a definite shape, thins, goes away.
  The smeared
church gives tongue. Not up, survivors lean on elbows

and feel aches. Yesterday, Eve of the Unblessed,
rain slanted, market awnings strained, chrysanthemums
grown here for the dead were left unsold. The seller
huddled in her sleeves. Asked, Do you believe

in God? the bearded novelist replied, "At
night sometimes." But never at all "shall these dead rise,"
unsold. Today, day of still visiting the dead, then drink,
scented bronze blooms on to their faded eyes.

Many grave flowers, I say, in yesterday's storm were left
unsold. Today, day of still visiting the dead, then drink,
religious half-seas-over, how we seem old, our kind,
our whole kind I mean, how old, old we seem.

Master of Aleatory Verse

Because MacOssian thieves what other men have written
Detested bullying Englishmen abuse him.
Why not, when only reiving
Lallans-leaking Scots excuse him?

Humble Admission?

His book, in its green jacket, has lain for a year
on my stone table. I have been into it, and come out,
put it down again, neglected it,
accusing me.

                    I loved him. Yes,
but my trouble is, he has grown — should I say — too
wise for me? That I can't pass the lake
to his last cavern? That the blue valley
between his high baroque cloister and cloister
intimidates me, too immense for striding?

Or could it be, he bores me now?
And in his green jacket lies there now
on a cold table, I repeat, accusing?

After the Assassination of Martin Luther King

Walking by William Morris's Kelmscott, leaves
   on thin trees greening along the river,

My children ahead just visible by a white
   bridge, I think of that good man shot, still

Not buried, and notice how long and black, black is
   my coated shadow on the harrowed grass.

Because it is black, shoot
   at my long shadow, malignant fools.

Through your blind telescopic sights shoot
   the black shadow of my head.

Unfashionable, Unlugubrious Thoughts of Venice

Moments recur which are time's pure poules de luxe, I say,
by Titian undressed, set by Tiepolo on clouds, demi-
goddesses yet not on sale to those who have the cash.

How these moments taste
I could now indicate, how too
they touch, the expensive scent they wear, how
their colours, shapes combine in as I say
delighted moods or modes of most
magnificent painters.

        But (though you say, they
are no recompense, though I reply, Well,
they happen, and recur) at this moment it's
these moments' analogues in sound
that I prefer — viz., their nature's a soprano
soaring
with no strain inside its strength, rocking
a little also, higher than roofs,
higher than swifts, in grace, in coloured
campanile air more slow. Or these moments'
nature is husky pure sound from stiff
long clarinets
        You smile at this,
remembering the young clarinettist I professed
to love, who played towards tourist lovelies
in the square, plump, resembling Tintoretto's
Balliol-educated Satan tempting Christ.

He played. He turned his wrist and looked, the notes
still coming, at his watch, to know how soon,
his playing over, moments might recur.

(I saw that in the cathedral too, at the high
non-moment of the mass, a server, young,
turning his wrist round to his watch,
terrestrial; blue incense on the air.)

Two Love Poems

1
Brilliant Flowers on a White Plate, at Breakfast

Duncovitch the philosopher
Lived in a barrel throughout winter,
In spring and summer was head waiter,
Entered, town-crying "Marmalada!",
Laid on your plate alone — quite right,
Since you were like a picture — purple
Curved anthers of the Caper.

2
Grotto, And Recollection

I swam from you through the grotto, it was not cold,
Under its black roof to the far rock, wrote
On the rock treading water your initial with
One finger,
Swam back to you: your small
Stiff nipples
I remember.

The Swing

The empty swing in the garden
Moves backwards, forwards,

Back, then forward,
Hidden a moment by its tree trunk
On each diminishing sway,
Our child who swung there crying
Having slipped off, and gone away.

Up, and Down

As this wall adds up, flint
to flint fitted,
red shapes
fall to the hot flints
in the hot sun.

Let us precisely state
they are petals of
coquelicot,
poppy in our
cross-channel tongue,

Red excessively,
which are falling
one, then one,
then together, two,
in the hot sun.

End of Our Summer

Hard brisk wind from our sea: it makes
Everything shudder. Hard dull
Red rock: it is harder
From absence of light. In this

Hollow here we make our
Last picnic in France, cold
In the mouth, in this north, drink
Wine we brought from the south.

All the best picnic places
Were taken: that slope by
The ford: you said here, you said there,
I said no, I drove on, you were

47

Cross. So we reached
This last hollow at last where
Our child pulls at pinks which
Are brown; where I break a baguette,

Where you hold your stainless
Steel mug and you suddenly say there's
Some warmth after all in this chill;
Where I button my mac, and agree;

Where comes harmony suddenly back —
You lean back, on the ling,
At this edge, this hard ledge
Of our northern leaden whipped sea.

Seasonal Uneasy Poem

September, how it rains,
how uneasy swallows
flick their white
bellies through wet
green-barricaded black
hollows of our hearts,
uneasy swallows
who reject September.

Yahoos: A Variation and Reply

I think I love the human race.
Queer though its ways and queer its face,
Queer though it Elvises, its Stans, its Rons,
Its Christian exegetes, its dons,
It has pros as well as cons.
True it is by me's and you's
Are burnt both Vietnamese and Jews.
True that its pros seem hard to find.

But never mind:
Short as you may suppose their list,
Sour pessimist,
They do exist, they do exist.

I Love You

That an American soldier should offer
a mug of cool, cool water, or
lukewarm, lukewarm water,
to a child only singed by
the petroleum jelly which other Americans
have dropped, accords with
the decencies of our nurture, no doubt,

but that a photograph of him doing it
should be "released", to show how kind
of course American soldiers are, and so
how just is this American war and how
excusable it is to burn (incidentally — how
did I forget to say it? — "war is a nasty
business") human or other animals of any
age, whether the young or old,

is an act of a backward country
where most things, decencies included,
are priced, and pushed by salesmen,
and are mostly sold.

Mass Media's Media

Let's play —
  Paper boats, paper boats under the bridge
With Barbara Cartland and Muggeridge,

Anthony Burgess, Auberon Waugh,
And Levin and Stevas and five or six more.

Let's watch —
   Stevas smirking from strength to strength,
   Brophy still leading by half a length,

   Auberon floating from sneer to sneer
   And Brophy la Belle going over the weir

   And old B. Nichols and old G. Winn
   And Allsop stuck where the drains come in,

   For all of these bleeders
   It's sink or swim,

And I'm sad to say —
   When they've all of them gone
   The drains like the river will still run on.

Old Man by a Lake in June

He stands, knees bent, against copper-blue.

His red singlet is brief: you can see
grey pubic hairs curling over his fallen flesh,
his thighs hollow under a loose freckled old skin.

He has folded his clothes by a white bench, laid
his cloth cap on them at the foot
of a muscular plane tree. He climbs
carefully trying to be certain, pulling the rail.

Balances — how shrunken he is. Dives, from
ten feet, breaks reflections of mountains, swims
with long easy strokes, arms thrusting
ahead of his head, as if he were young, past brown
children the town instructor is teaching to swim.

  It is hard to climb out,
but at last he stretches at length on his towel,

adjusts his cloth cap over his eyes and sleeps
before lunch, if you call it sleep, his last summer,
it wouldn't surprise me, under the mountains,
under the freckling sun.

Old also, I wish him no thinking, only
the feel of the sun.

To Wystan Auden
On his birthday, February 21, 1967

Now for your sixtieth birthday am I to send you
a long card which is sparkly with greetings?
　Well I might. Or I might in the dark tonight
light sparklers and wave them round in
your honour. Forty years have gone by since I read
a first poem of yours, since you emerged out
of England's life, and her centuries, out of Long Mynd
and her midlands, a poet, also a teacher, in the decentest
sense of the words a "superior person".
("Of course, Grigson, you have only to be with him,
Nicholson, Moore, or MacNiece, a short while,"
the old novelist said — I was young – "to know
they are most superior persons.")
　On TV lately I have seen you amble away
through your orchard under the Alps, seen
your face, wizened, wise, I would say,
slowly divide to a smile benignly lacking
conceit. But I shall not today bow to Tu Fu
in his mountains. Excuse me, instead if I
interfere in your early family concerns and imagine
a choleric baby, wizened, red,
held over a font, and a shell raised, water dribbled,
a voice then in Anglican accent pronouncing "I name
this child Wystan." (That you bawled
would be likely : ex post facto I'm certain in dudgeon
the devil sneaked off through the door.)

51

Excuse me again if I turn to Thomas of Marlborough,
abbot of Evesham, and read what he says of this
minor saint of our midlands, Wigstan or
Wystan, grandchild of the King of the Men
of the Border — not that you are a saint, I hurriedly say
to save you more and more awkward disclaimer, no one
knowing better than you, though saints may be poets,
poets most seldom are saints.
            No, but according to Thomas, as you
are aware, this young Wigstan was kissed with
a kiss of peace and then a sword flew, and where
his head of fair hair hit the Wistanstow
field, most strongly, strangely, a pillar of light
came down and stayed there.

By luck, you were named well, and I honour you now
you've honoured us by your love these long years, still
your head pretty fly on its shoulders. I'm thankful
to say, still in our darkness by rughe knokled knarres
off Main Street, off High Street, by grike
and by fell, an extra fine light, though you
will disclaim that as well.

Note on Grünewald

Even if ten of my poems should be read in ten hundred
    years' time,
I'd sooner, kind readers, thank you, myself
be around, in spite of aspirations and all
pious aere perennius asseverations, to sniff
in the month appropriate, as once
for instance in the hot street with-
in distance of Grünewald's spotted green-rotted Christ,
            the scent of the flowers of lime.

So I join, at least today, morning of glitter in December
our poet Cowper, who decided as he watched the leaves
    of
his whole county falling in a shower of yellow,

that shortness of staying in this Vale of Tears, for all
his madness and his swingeing fears, ceased
to attract him: he would leave this world never,
he would enjoy, in spite of idealisms and moral realisms,
the good of it for ever, and ever.

This Third Person Will Not Do

Her bare feet, her knees,
I hear the now regular huskiness
of her breathing,
feel her breath on me,
my right arm over the cooled cornice
of her shoulder.

This third person will not do.
I speak of two. So
for *hers* read *yours* all through,
speaking of you.

Vintage on the Loir

Wines rest in cold caves, becoming clear and fine,
says monsieur in his book, and look how each
vent of warm wind shakes down a yellow
patter of wandering leaves, across their

Chalky mouths, to which
come grapes as Pol de Limbourg
painted them in black patched barrels —
listen to trickling from the press,

A spring of wine: sniff, a most awkward
word, but sniff, a sweet scent
comes out, of most new, most aboriginal
life, O ancient lie, from underground.

Rose Disintegrating

The petals of my particular rose have fallen,
The carmine at their edges curling
At one end crinkles into white,
They spill over a dead newspaper of this morning.
Don't look at them. Let's go.
Switch off the light.

Red Dahlias

To vanish, after a share,
if not enough, of the
yellow fruits of the world,
sharp, scented and sweet, without

Pain or too much pain to
those I love and leave.
But I wake up again:
more of a white winter's

Orb tops our north-
facing cliff, condensation
shapes skulls on
each rectangular pane,

Noises return, and
though early months were
this year cold and fruits are
few, how most outrageously,

Were I to look down
through these skulls, could I
discern the red rough way, next
door, their dahlias burn.

Andrew Young, Recalling April, 1964

Ancient igneous stone, not exactly
erratic, heat locked not cold in him,
loyal to his living, eyes
under eyebrows of lichen
not at all dim.

Had climbed a mountain, Sliabh
in Scotland, two years ago, at seventy-seven,
"Older than Wordsworth
when he made a last
climb of Helvellyn."

Laughed: up went his lichenous eyebrows,
was his age for a while. Then said,
did I mind — must go
to his room for a second, must
water his head.

Came back. Laughed again. Often do that for
headaches, head needs a wetting. Spoke
of Hardy and Patmore,
laughed again, drank whisky,
complained of forgetting.

Seventy-nine: this tramp of a man,
hard fire-centred stone,
had travelled for miles to see,
for reasons if known, not
at all to be shown,

Once again a circle of stone,
gone out, stood there again,
as if not alone (for a reason
of heart, it's my guess) in this
driving, kniving cold rain.

Tollund Man

Upper Norwood of neatness, where Pissarro
took refuge and painted the Crystal Palace, has
spread long ago into Jutland: heath has retreated,

bogs have been cut, suburbs extended, he has been
found, not a bearded old French-Jewish painter but
simply a neighbour? Twisting a plaiting

of leather knotted his life out, fed by rite
on dry seeds, flung in sodden-weed winter
to grow in black earth, a gift

for the Goddess of Growing grasping
her belly, for her being in spring,
gaily-served — or they say so — great exacting

Mama of Increase; then exhumed, then examined,
kept out of wet, black, in a case,
in a Jutland museum, focused —

they tramp all the time up the suburban
creak of the stairs — through huge-hooded
lenses by teachers of physical culture (wives

looking on, not at him) from violent
Dallas, eaters of Natural Foods on a
Fairy Tale Tour of H-C-Andersen Land:

No consolation after millenia, my friend,
sacrificed for a future, to stir in this way
by your shiny, silky-black shape; your

fluidity hardened, more natural than
Lenin; your stomach post-mortem'd; head cut from
your body; like ours, your finger-prints taken.

Exceptional Bird, At Last Visible

Supposing he stayed until these ultimate leaves
were dropping, flitting verdigris in our damp
valley through mists of the morning —
        O supposing he stayed, even
all-shooting Sunday hunters would not shoot him.

Poems by Pierre de Ronsard about his Valley

1. From "Praises of Vendômois"

O happy land,
    The Muses' home is here
Bright with the beauty
    Of the sky and year.

On you with hand unsparing
    From their full store
Happiness and plenty
    All their favours pour.

The two slopes which immure you
    Are strong and do not fail
To protect you always
    From the grumbling gale.

Mother of demigods,
    On one the blest Gâtine
Raises to the sky
    Her painted head of green,

And on the other flourishes
    Grape-heavy vine on vine
Whose liquor need not envy
    The sweet Anjou wine.

57

The tardy Loir conducts
  Her most meandering flow
Of waters through your meadows
  Bright as they are slow,

Making with the humour
  Distilled from its fat mud
All the land it travels through
  Very rich and good.

2. Gastine of Demigods

  Gastine of demigods, sweet secretary
Of my distress, who answers in the high
Or low singing of your trees
The long sighs my heart's not able to suppress;
  Loir, halting the strong running of the streams
Which tumble through our Vendômois
To hear me rounding on that loveliness
With which I cannot satisfy my emptiness;
  Suppose the auguries were rightly read, suppose me
Right about yesterday's sweet
Looks from my sweet Thalia,
  Then making me a poet, death or no,
You will be named by France the one
My bays, the other my Castalia.

3. Ode on Choosing His Sepulchre

  Caves, and you
  Springs who glide
  Down from these
    Superior rocks;

  Forests, waters, who
  Wind among these
  Fields, banks, woods,
    Listen to my voice.

When Heaven and my hour
Decide my death and snatch
Me from the sweet sojourn of
   Our common day,

I wish, require, command,
That the tomb given me shall
Not be built near kings, or be
   Engraved in gold,

But set on this green island
Which the half-seen embracing
Current of the Loir
   Curls round,

There where its never-
Sleeping darling Braye
Comes to its lap
   Murmuring.

I declare, no one
Shall carve marble in desire
To add a pride of beauty
   To my tomb.

For shade, don't
Give me marble but a tree
That will be all
   And always green.

Let earth engender ivy
Out of me, which shall
Wind round me
   Turn on turn;

And let my sepulchre
Be decorated with a twisting
Vine which throws a dispersed
   Shade around.

Shepherds, with their flocks,
Shall come there on the fête
Ordained for me
  Each year;

And when they have paid
The sweet devoir of their sacrifice
They will address my island,
  They will say:

"You are famous as the
Appointed tomb of one
Whose poems shall be heard
  By all the world,

"Who never felt the sear
Of envy in his day, never
Sucked up for honours
  To great men,

"Never gained love
By philtres or made
Research in tricks of
  Antique sorcery.

"But rather showed us in our
Fields the Muses' sisterhood
Treading the grass to
  His songs' harmony,

"For he drew such
Music from the lyre
That his songs graced
  Our meadows and ourselves!

"Let manna drop
Gently always on his tomb,
With that sweet humour
  Nights of May produce!

"All round may grass
And sounding water fold him,
One always rippling, and
    One always green!

"And in remembrance of his fame
And glory shall we pay him
Such honours every year
    As Pan received."

The band of shepherds will
Say this, then each one will pour
A bowl of young lamb's blood
    And milk

To me, who at that time
Shall share the orchard
Where the Elysian
    Spirits live,

Where hail and snow
Lack footing and where
No thunderbolts
    Strike down,

But all green growth
Maintains immortal green
And every season keeps the
    Happiness of spring.

Zephyr blows there
On myrtles and a plain
Which has the colours of
    A thousand flowers.

Not driven by thirst
And not enticed by kings
To spoil the world
    For power,

These spirits live
As brothers there following
In death such callings as they
   Knew in life.

There, there, I say, will
Alcaeus play his angry lyre to me,
Sappho will sing more gently
   Than the rest,

And those who listen
To the odes which
Pour from them
   Will thrill to hear

Sweet varied harmonies
Which makes even the one
Who rolls that stone
   Forget his pain!

Only the sweet lyre, only
The lyre dispels the sorrows
Of our hearts, affording
   Solace to the ear.

4. *Against the Woodmen of the Forest of Gâtine*

Rest your arm, woodman; they are not
trees you're tumbling to the ground. There's blood
there, look, blood oozing drop by drop from
nymphs who were alive below the toughness
of that bark. Sacrilegious murderer,
if thieves who steal loot not worth a threepenny
piece get hanged, then shouldn't stake and faggots,
irons, deaths, tortures, be visited on you,
you evil man, who kill our goddesses?

Forest, high home of woodland birds,
the solitary stag and the light roe-deer will no more

graze in your shadows; and your green mane
will scatter light of the summer sun no more
and the amorous shepherd no more lean
against a tree and blow into his four-holed flageolet,
his sheepdog at his feet, his crook beside him,
and speak of the ardours of his fair Janette.
All will be mute, Echo will lose her voice:
you will be fields, and where your trees
stand now, whose broken shade stirs slowly,
you'll feel the share, the coulter and the plough; you'll
    lose
your silence, lose your Satyrs and your Pans, the does
will no more hide their fawns in you.

Goodbye, old forest, toy of the God
of the Light Wind, where I first tuned my lyre;
where I first heard the humming arrows
of Apollo, who came and filled my whole heart
with wonder; where I admired the fair Calliope, and so
first turned lover of her band of nine, when
her hand showered a hundred roses on my brow
and when Euterpe suckled me with her own milk.

Goodbye, old forest, goodbye, you sacred heads,
revered so long with tablets and with flowers,
who can no longer shield with your sweet cool
greenery the thirsty traveller from the burning air
who looks and finds you gone, accuses those
who murdered you, and goes grumbling on.

Goodbye, oaks, with which brave citizens are crowned,
Jupiter's trees, Dodonian seedlings, who gave
their first food to those ungrateful beings,
men, who will not recognize the benefits
they've had of you, brute-beings to massacre
their foster-fathers as they do!

Misfortune waits for that man who trusts in men!
O Gods, how accurate is that philosophy
which says that all things pass away, at last,
and meanwhile only change their form!

The Vale of Tempe will be a peak
some day, the Mount of Athos will be one wide plain,
Neptune will one day wave with corn:
always the substance stays, the form is lost always.

Travelling at Night
(after Tu Fu)

Delicate grasses ashore
stir in a small wind. Tall
my boat's mast in this
night's loneliness. Stars
depend to these
wide wide levels.

A moon dances on this great
river's rippling.

Writing gives me no name,
illness, age, bar my advancement —
drifting, drifting
here, what am I like
but a tern of the sandbanks
in between earth
and heaven?

Sixteen Dogs, Cats, Rats and Bats
(for Sophie)

Sixteen dogs and sixteen cats
Went chasing after sixteen rats.
The sixteen rats were full of fear
And wished that they were bats, in air.
No sooner wished than so they were,
The sixteen rats were sixteen bats
Safe above all dogs and cats,

And to and fro, and fro and to,
About the sky each night they flew,
Leaving the sixteen cats to howl
And the sixteen dogs to growl.

They did not like it in the sky
Where all their food was moth or fly,
They had no cheese, they licked no butter,
They slept behind a leaky gutter
Upside down, as all bats sleep,
And now they wished once more to creep
In rat-shape round a rubbish heap.

No sooner wished than they were down
Dragging their tails around the town
And sixteen dogs and sixteen cats
At once appeared and ate those rats.

Moral: Better be a living bat
Than line the stomach of a cat.

Occasion

Sunrise.

Briefly most ordinary
Insects are fireflies.

The cliff stays black.

Polished apples on smooth blue,
In scarlet, are
Amazingly embossed.

So far, so far no killing
Of the frost.

Academic Affair

They're separately old — it would be thirty
Spring terms ago they met,
The lectured to, and that spruce
Lecturer on Eng. Lit.

I wonder still what set him, in her digs,
Above her tongue to tongue.
He lectured, he was handsome, — well,
The girl at least was young,

But when she walked she plunged,
She had no grace.
She had — later, it's true — an avid
Look upon that ugly face.

It wasn't fair to call her,
As some did, a bitch;
On heat — though always kind — she always was,
She looked a witch.

Still avid, plunging, knowing,
And obscenely frisky,
Today she peps on students
And rye whisky,

While iron-grey-haired, emeritus,
Urbane and rather witty.
He's called to chair each
Save our Youth committee.

I've seen and known
The other men, the weedy ones she took,
And wondered what man her first man really was
Below that military intellectual look.

Five Brief Notes for The Downward Year

1. Climax

Eyes amazed with brightness
of these curled orange
arils of wild iris.

2. Musical Climax

Black music of thirteen birds,
preening, waiting, the length of
five phone wires.

3. Poetry Reading

Michaelmas, our Miss Millay
recites Gascoyne in
a women's college.

4. Mont Saint-Michel
Attained

Up high I step off rungs
to battlements, shakily
across high tide.

5. Painting by Bombois

Storing apples, O gross thighs
of that *grosse fermière*
sur une échelle.

Harshness of Insistent Seasons

I will remind you that the Seasons
governed us, on mucky altars and in pits
of blood. Mosaics, painted arches,
carols, books of hours.

Sowing and riding out to meet the May,
revering the last sheaf, shaking
patter of acorns down for swine,
drying wet feet at November sticks,
made idle coldly by the ice and snow
(we warmed — see Pol de Limbourg's Hours —
clothes lifted, bed behind, our male
and female members at that fire).

So on and on, so less and less,
until — we're clever — we could make
these Months and Seasons blur. Until
we chucked out gods, such broken cups
and spent torch batteries, in
our bins backdoor.

      Now that was good,
a poor conceited arbitrary arrogant
crouching bullying, if at times poetic
band of mixed-up, blood-desiring
brats, occasionally kind, ourselves
not gods (who no gods need), they were.

So, exit some,
though not all fear.

But then, Pyrrha, Deucalion, Adam, Eve,
Good Soldier Schweik, le bon Fouterre,
Miss World, and England's Queen,
why are we here?

Distress reduced, can skinny Metaphysic
now be drowned
(let's hope it can)
in Metaphysic's ancient beer?

Poems 1970—1974

Dead Poets: Recalling Them in November

Friends, my friends of so much
Time gone, of languages
Brighter than mackerel,
It is beyond bearing that you are dead.

No, I bear it most days too easily.
But there are moments when a drop falls
And sends tremors over my bason, at 8 a.m.
When light comes up behind

Our hill and reveals flaws in the
Window-glass shaped like comets or
Skulls: to think of you warm, of you gone
Is a cold air all round me then.

So many. And in so many ways
Of course myself I mourn, my
Own ash throw on to that
Frosty grey lawn.

May Immediately: No Memoirs

I fight to see round light
of a rounding, then straight
light of a rapidly straight falling
drop of rain: changing

From noticing May days
to noticing November, I say
"I will use
with freshness only,

If at all, *again* —
no memoirs, please." I fight
I can't suppose of course
successfully, *remember*.

He-Dove

I regard as well the Collared Dove,
he is the Levantine Dove,
he has pushed north,
he wears a black collar.

He says deka okto:
in Greek he compares
the franc and the pound and the mark
and the dollar.

Then out of leaves
he flies over our garden
and as he flies
he squeaks like a weak

Cat. Enough of that:
this dove with a collar
inclines to the modes
and the mores

Of the High Tories
or the Wood Pigeon:
he is not the She-Dove
of my religion.

Scullion

Blue eyes, red red nose, and bright
ginger hair: on the pavement
opposite goes one of our Bruegel world
without much to be glad of, I fear.

He decides on this bitter March morning not
to wait for a bus up the street,
so as well I observe how he minces
on peculiar points of long feet.

Also I see he has hands with
outsticking knuckles as red as his nose,
and I imagine him in the year 1400
cold in old ill-fitting hose:

The old word for him was a scullion,
cutting the castle meats,
this kitchen hand ashore from a liner,
this sad cockatoo whatever he eats.

Our Bruegel race has its jokes,
I can only say it's not fair
to combine such blue, red and white and sharp
feet and such hair. I say, it's not fair.

Incident of Wolves and Water

Two men saw two long wolves cross low
   From the extensive forest which no more
Exists and go into the also now vanished church,
   Ruined most of it, by an unhinged sagging door.

Two men saw on their hind legs on the earth floor
   These same wolves lap from its pillared marble bowl
Stale holy water as if (they thought) beasts
   Of the devil as well needed medicament for the soul.

No more than this incident of wolves and water
   Is recalled of that church whose footing grates a
   plough,
No yob of piety mentions that the same black bowl,
   unpillared,
   Affords drink in a near yard to fat pigs, now.

Scent of Women

Peculiar the scent of wood anemones,
they smell like sweat of aestuous women,
bitter, green. Each year I enter
a copse where these fox-flowers grow.

For their exquisiteness I go, then
think of women I never loved, and feared,
too soon thinking of the cyclamen.

Alexander and the Talking Tree
(after a miniature to Firdawsi's Shahnama)

Wrong connection ringing 999
(A.D.) Firdawsi here in Khorasan, sun
High in fount of lapis lazuli,
Larks up also high, above

Our roses' bed: Sikandar
Scans at this or his world's end or edge
Antelope, ocelot, ox instead, each
Cut off head stuck on a Talking Tree.

Never like him question a Talking Tree,
Which is not consolatory. Tell it
Or not, it knows your name. It shrieks.
At noon, at midnight, scented

Musk, from leaves of either trunk
You hear your name. This vegetable
Always knows your name, and says
The same; mutters the mutual hate

Of men, that you'll be dead, consigns
To pattern, or patter, sun up high
In lapis lazuli, and larks, stuffed
Larks, over our roses' bed.

In View of the Fleet

It was most grey: a mob of birds wheeled
through gelid air and went away: cold grey
became the habit of the day.

Lying in bed, it was small-fingered Hardy
thinking of the dead I thought about; and things
which prompted what he said.

A hedgehog on his lawn, a gypsy's infant
sodden in a ditch, still-born, another, then
another such indifferent dawn.

No hope, within the circle
of the telescope a hanged man dangling
at the end of a rope.

The same, always the same. A child
playing his violin again to a handcuffed
convict waiting for the train.

Things not as firstly well, a sparkling day, and
tolling of a bell. Then,
the second death as well.

Take what comfort we can along the bent wind-
worn blackthorn of man. Yes, in our lea
what comfort we can.

So I must think it true that for the moment
it comforted you to see, past your thorn, your still
Fleet's long tape of blue.

Though you might see and say that the hunched
man-thorn rooted in sliding clay twists always
away from that most azure bay.

Sod F.R.S. Synthesizes the People's Opium

In a communication to *Nature* my old friend Sod
Announced that he and his colleagues, fellows
Of Corpus, had synthesized God.

Careful at first, priests now applaud,
They propose we partake, as if it were snuff, of Sod's new
White crystals of Risen Lord.

What they don't understand is that bloody old Sod
In *Nature* next week will dilate on the rather un-
Pleasant side-kicks from God.

In bulk by compulsion dyed a bright orange
God should be had, he will say, on prescription
Alone in a fish-shaped lozenge.

I think I must add that having in this way synthesized God
And started a really stupendous addiction, his conscience
Is pricking old Sod.

To get us back on the level
He's begun work, has old Sod, on
Synthesized Devil.

Homily

*(The Space Director reads from his reading pulpit over the
tonsured heads of his Masters of Science, who do not speak
as they feed.)*

Today I read — he begins to intone —
Of a sullen dwarf who lived in a stone.

Last dwarf in his ancient land, this dwarf alone
Remembered the nine cures for iron driven into the bone.

An M.I.T. warlock, who also alone
Remembered the nine lays for drawing dwarfs out of stone,

Had just drawn that timid sullen dwarf out of his stone,
With a moan,

When neighbours caught him on his knees, by the stone,
And shot Christian iron-headed arrows into his bone,

And he pitched dead on his face in front of the stone,
And without giving, this last dwarf ran like a rabbit back
  into his stone,

The which per saecula saeculorum had been, and would
  be,
Henceforth, for ever and ever, his home.

Amen. Amen.

Sir P.B. Publico

His lips are lines, his mouth
  Is not quite straight,
He has made large legal earnings
  In a mystique of the state,
So in his enamelled nook lives
Old, and sheltered now because
"His public services" — un-
  Doubtedly — "were great."

Well-bred, finally affronted
  By his need to die,
He used to make the uncritical
  Young accept his fortified lie,
And go and fight across
  Our globe — and so assuage
His jealousy a year or two
  — And die.

They were heroes, if his opposite number's
  Napalm entirely burned them;
They were a nuisance, if the mouth
  Of jagged death returned them.
Or if they had wisely dodged,

Sir Publico's disciples for
Ever after tried
    To make us spurn them.

If young men shit now, between his wars,
    With less reserve on his designs,
Publico, P.C., C.H., and K.B.E.,
    Enumerates their crimes
Still in that comic evil
Dialect, which Publicos
Preserve for writing
    Letters to *The Times*:

Self-satisfied young bullies
    If they fail to find apartheid funny.
Unwashed, long-haired, without
    Respect for money,
Idle, because they'd like,
Before they are old, and
Twisted in the mouth,
    Their taste of honey.

For ever graciously he pushes round
    Port at the High Table,
Drops, to likelier, sounder
    Young, hints of his Sacred Fable,
Recruits new sub-
Contractors to maintain
The battlements on his domestic
    Tower of Babel.

★   ★   ★

Dryden, I've never cared much for your
    Politics, but you were wise,
Each year, you wrote, new
    Maggots make new flies,
And so — you spoke of fools,
I speak of knaves — this old,
Perhaps needed, native
    Species never dies.

Courtanvaux

The waisted Russian dancers float
under great trees
and float and float and turn.

All disappears, white pigeons
rise away, the waisted dancers multi-
coloured sing, and float, and turn, and sway.

Their level song. Foxgloves and ices, fires,
cherries, and cornflowers and carnations. Under
great trees beyond

Tall urns these colours float, all else
beyond, behind they float, footless
they turn, they float away.

Downward white birds return,
round them thin branches
also slightly sway.

These dancers turn, these waisted Russian
footless ones, these tall multi-
colours, float and float

And sing and turn
slowly and sway, straining our white
Sundayness their way.

Trôo, July 1970

A Letter Occasioned by Finishing,
on a Morning of My 66th June
(and after Hearing of the Death of E.M. Forster),
City Without Walls

Wystan, I write to you
From a high terrace,
Having, as I waited for guests,
Read all your book.
Roses are out, which grew
From our cuttings, white roses
Frame our veranda,
From a scabbed tree,
Dead, hang pink roses
Deepening to red. Of
Jerusalem Sage yellow
Hooks up-curl at our door.
With high trees, below,
This country
Is Pierre de Ronsard's,
Enclosing his river.
A wind freshly wiffles
Through leaves where I write,
Sways white acacias,
Keeps the iron garden
Table cool to my
Hesitant forearm.

Later from poplars
May ascend voices exciting
As well unease a little —
Of orioles,
Jubilant birds
In secrets of leaves.
But again, again
Am I grateful!

It is not far past these
Lombardy trees that Ronsard,
With toothache, and deaf,

And yellow with ague,
Wrote of his hope
That an orangey scent
(Oranges were rare in his day)
Might rise from his verses.
Such too is your fragrance,
White warlock,
From the vorgebirge of Austria or
From heavy Manhattan: if I could,
I would now wholly, without
Afterthoughts, or those thoughts
You write of (but alone
In the margin) which come when
We elderly wake in the night,
Say, by your rhythm,
I am glad to be living.

What is grace all the same
Which I, but less strongly,
Discern, you proclaim: again
Your hand is in blessing. It is
Something after these years
To be of your blest; you
Seeing, rejecting, in
Room Thirty or writing
Our extra
Betrayal and torture.

Bauchant near our valley
(Gallo-Roman, of ancient
Names and emotion, where
Christ in a mandorla
Shines in exquisite violet
In the wet church
Alongside our mill,
If the west door is
Opened at sunset —
Though on the motte
Which masters the valley
Catholics cooked Protestants,

Protestants Catholics in turn,
A petit feu, by the record)
Dreamed fêtes with flags
In a ripple, chariots
Charging in races
Under the chalk happiness
Dancing, to a song
Of pure France; and painted
His flowers. Should he not
Paint them, though real
In a jug of *cul noir*
Or stiff
In his paint of a lyric,
Flowers could not soothe,
After all, in their far
Removed house his dotty wife
Screaming and moaning?

Then I introduce to you,
Wystan, Montrouveau
Up on the hill:
Where pansies extend into gravel
From borders of tyres:
For his friends there and neighbours
Ronsard our friend called
On their saint, in a hymn.

Listen, Monsieur St-Blaise,

Let no fire infect them,
No mad dogs fang them,
No wolves leer and leap
On their sheep
From Gastines. Let their
Girls find their men,
Let grapes on their vines
Swell tight every season,
Udders vastly distend,
Fat cheese on their platters
Of willow depend

82

Good Monsieur and friend,
In Heaven,
Now kindly attend.

I write to the curé:
No one in this village,
He replies sadly for not
Quite my reason, sings
Or remembers, in these days,
Their hymn.

Feeling with,
None the less — that is also
Your forte, none
Are excluded, not even
Yourself, brown
Wrinkled walnut, wry
Self-commentator;
Not one of our selves, with our
Years in our faces
Who also forget in a
Fear to look forward;
Not the young coming after.

   Green pillows of cress
In the brook which begins us
You celebrate too;
And up from your verses,
Though many
Forget them, stinking
Ogres not read them,
Blest by high priests
Stiff generals not
Stoop to reject them,
Rises an odour
Of essence, I say, of
Ripeness and rareness.

Thanks be, these fruits
Ripen still on
Your tree, although fruit
Has to fall, although
Cypresses blacker
Than shade, yet
Scented as well
(Save to those who lie under),
In their ranks and their ranks
Rise over the wall.

Trôo, June 1970

Great Curassow

Your eyes gleam: by post
has arrived something you wrote for,
its wrappings around you
you sit up in bed. Your temperature's down,

Yes, you will get up after lunch. Meanwhile
stamps, tweezers, album,
a Great Curassow, a blue iris
on yellow, Oh

You finger the secret,
child, child, I enfold you, love you
and hold you. If I had the power it is
now, since I know what I know,

O now in the gleam of your eyes you might
suddenly, Magyar Posta,
blue iris on yellow, cease
in your glow.

Mulberry Castle, or National Trust

Branches most heavy with black berries
hang over cars, parked. And berries
fall. Rooted their tree below sweet
turf fitting, round upthrust

Chunks of ugly wall, exactly
a space where kings, we may suppose like us
more often sour, queens unwilling
usually (Lycett-Green-dressed snake

Courtiers crawling round) pre-acted scenes,
or takes, of this and that,
poor actors; were the Lord's Anointed,
cold, mean, allowing no one near.

The fire, red-nosed snot-swallowers
with catarrh, haunted by fear in bed,
on throne, on seats of necessaria
of draughty stone, whimperers or

Cruel, to be executed executioners,
meanwhile fly-chasers, racers of snails,
arse-licked by Lord's Anointers; sippers
of bad wines of Bordeaux, by tuneless

Trumpeters welcomed, trotting on sneak's
purposes of state or fate on wet
May Day. *Orangery, this way:*
Tenpence a frilled factory cake; sixpence

Grey-brown tea; in the place
provided, pee. Wipe the damned
mulberries from the roof and boot,
leave their swart stains

To the rain and check your oil,
and drive away, arriving teasy, tired,
and late, stuffed with
these glories of our blood and state.

Short History of Old Art
(for B.N.)

Masters, your vision's over-realized:
I look, I see one
of those details from your paintings
we enlarge which occupy extents
maybe two inches square
the far side of a martyrdom
or of the donkey's felt-tipped ear.

Most daylight's done. What light is left
reduces fuss, like you insists
on form, and I see air create round
smudged-on objects (trees without blue,
devoid almost of green),
in rhythm, a small
actual "especial scene".

In this extreme actuality — well, yes,
one facet of a spire is shaded, one facet's
caught a glow. This is, I realize,
that Absolute of All
you felt, in your theology
could not quite know, yet were all
but first — in miniature — to show.

Benediction of reality — there's something to it,
meaning for a moment things, or vice-
versa, are as real as me
or you, in which repose
it was imagined tall blessed ones did dwell,
did walk this side the water from that ripe
mouth of hell.

There's something to it, as I say:
it seldom comes, and luckily it can't
be held, air thickens, rhythm breaks, light
grows too grand or disappears. Outside our gallery
would I say luckily again, we
play dodge 'em with our fears, and dull
the red mouth reappears.

Raw Ream: Remembering, Now Dead, a Teacher

I speak of times before high whining of cars or round
growling of planes, when silence was fashioned by noises:
it is a pool in our hollow of pines looped by the sun
which makes them the colour of foxes, is defined
lightly by crows passing over, by
a huckling of hens relieved of their eggs,
by women calling to women, is broken, so
made by clangs, or by regular bells now and then.

Carrying white eggs for payment
I walk to you over the green
to learn reading, hearing this
sunshine of silence. Minnie, I say, these eggs
are my money. You laugh, take the eggs
(which you will give back to my mother),
skin ream off a pan, spread for me honey
on bread, yellow ream over honey.

Return to Florence

A theatre-sky, of navy blue, at night:
traffic of the night, it darts, it screams,
it is straight swifts of night with lighted
eyes: upwards I read on a new building's

Face. Here P.B. Shelley wrote
Ode to the West Wind. Your poet, no. Nor
mine, yet say wind as he will or wind,
oh, I say willkommen, welcome, ben-

Venuto, oh, bienvenu; and I — I am
here again, after fourteen years: I-you.
I-you shall in a minute see the Duomo's
domino sides enormous up into the night,

I-you shall pass *our* latteria stroll — there,
that corner shop where, look, — for your
sake — the kind man scented my hair. Soon
must Il Bianco come into view,

The Loggia lighted, Dante again in the night,
reading, on walls. I-you. Sleeping. To swifts
of morning to-morrow waking. Dead and to come,
oh, welcome, willkommen, benvenuti, oh, bienvenus!

Discoveries of Bones and Stones

I

Certain bones are from other bones distinguished
as not being common bones,
such as plesiosaurus bones, or the skull
in this plain deal cupboard
(plug inserted, as a notice directs,
so that I see this skull's brown regularity) of
my name-saint — supposing my parents had
thought that way — of at any rate Geoffroi
Abbot of Savigny, founder or may be promoter
of Fountains in our country and Furness.

   This uncommon cranium (with a piece of the shirt
of Thomas of Canterbury) I find — how it pours —
in a modern church, having stopped to ring
the ferry over the Manche, which he crossed more
   slowly,
in case there's a strike.

   Such is the casualness of discovery.

II

On this same journey, inspired by that gentle
regularity of the cranium of my more or less
name-saint, I have, on the other hand, since tried to see
the uncommon skull of St Aubert;

a peculiarity more celebrated into which
Michael Archangel, Provost of Heaven,
stuck his annoyed finger leaving a hole, to remind
Aubert to build on that hoar rock in the waters
which Victor Hugo has named Cheops of the West.
   But the sacristan was on holiday. No one
had the key.

III

Also at Gruchy where dung among granite
persists, where sea, down, far down a pack animal's lane
between hills, between nettles
is a palpable vee of his blue, I find
the site of the natal home, as announced
by a rusty notice, of
Angelus Millet.

   Having just been pulled down, grey granite
stones lie around, which enclosed you, Master of
blue unexpected in squalor of sabots.

IV

Do not expect about these discoveries
conclusions or comments; on texts such as, pieties wear
   out,
Mister Order of Merit,
be the stones or the bones of the matter
never so uncommon; such as, works — Furness,
Mont–Saint–Michel, or the Angelus even — are better
than bones or a scatter of stones. Or, bones in
live flesh are better than scattered dry bones. Or
of course, all bones are bones.

Impossibly Away from Home

    Far, Mister T. Gray Hardy,
    from your madding
    crowd, they wanted crowd.

The *Metamorphoses* they read,
had bright mosaic
down their best room
laid, looked through elms
at rain, spoke in coarse British,
breaking Latin, to huge-fingered
workmen steaming in the rain,
storms dribbling on, storms
making wide crops flat, again.

Indoors felt their felt
slippers Venus, ah in colours
Venus, Dido, Orpheus, Bacchus (stocks
of wine as well as
always love were low).
So unenergetically they dreamt
of Rome, to which
all straight roads led, by
Dubris, through both Gauls,
impossibly
away from home.

Perhaps So

Too much is remembered,
It is time more was forgotten;
Let these peacocks outside Warwick Castle
Yell, peck and display, cinnamon,
Blue, green, black
And grey. That will do for today.

It is time for more to be covered
In deep soil, and to sink.
It is time for rather less to be printed
Or scattered through air, time for more
To be written again, by hand,
In black ink.

Too much is found,
It is time to tread, not to dig.
Let much more be lost through
Holes in our cotton pockets,
More spent on sherbet, and on the quick
Transcience of Roman candles and rockets.

Too much is told. Banish polymath Steiners
And seventy-seven other bright British Shiners,
Naturalists, archaeologists, publishers
of publications in parts,
Norman Mailer
And all long-winded farts,

To an artificial, not too get-at-able
Or too satellite isle,
At least for a while,
Beyond the blind side of the Moon,
And for our health and your Muses' health,
O strictest Apollo, may it be soon.

Two Poems from Victor Hugo's Four Winds of the Spirit

1. *The Stair*

I am made of marble and shadow,
I sink into night like
Black roots of a tree.
I listen; I am underground;
From down there I say to the thunder:
Wait! Not a sound.

Called poet, I am in the dumb
Night the stairway of mystery;
I am the stair named Dark; on the
Spiralling gloom of my fall
And rise Shadow opens
Her vague eyes.

The torches shall become tapers.
Keep away from my virginal steps,
Pass, gay crowd of the day! My stair
Is not built for the winged
Feet of holiday or the feet
Of love which are bare.

At my livid deep
Everything trembles, fear beads
Even the ghosts.
From the dead grave
I rose to this door, through which
A gleam shows.

The banquet is laughter and blaze.
On their throne of blood by the world
The gay masters are censed and
Served; and woman, against
Their mightiness,
Measures her nakedness.

Leave latch and key.
I am the stair; Grief
Broods; the hour will sound;
Someone whom shadows surround
Shall climb my dark steps,
Someone come down.

2. Near Avranches
(and in sight of Mont Saint-Michel, which was then a prison)

On the immensity of gloom the gloom of night was
    falling.

The wind of evening breathed, and with an anxious wing
sent scurrying over granite reefs a few
sails to harbour, a few birds to their nest.

Sad to the verge of death, I saw the world. How
huge the sea, how deep the soul of man!

Saint-Michel rose, Cheops of our West, pyramid
of the seas, by itself on its bitter tides.

I thought of Egypt wrapped by impenetrable folds,
of the great immortelle by itself in the sands,
black tent of the kings, that parcel of shadows asleep
in the motionless dark camp of the dead.
Alas. In these deserts which God, alone
in his wrath, alone in his leniency, fills with
vast breathing, man on the horizon has built
a tomb and a prison.

The Dying of a Long Lost Lover

Your mother slept with me — I daresay you regard that
as peculiar, I daresay she is old (and so am I,
but I'm less your affair). Think. She was young.
Imagine her. I see still her long fingers round her belt.

Which is her myth, her past, or her reality?
Young, did not foretell this old I do not know.
I know she is the hand which stroked both me and you:
various the occasions, and the kinds, of love she felt.

You touch that vehicle of extinct heat. But love
that she loved, and was the call of love. With some
distaste you soon may close her eyes: love
that I see her young long fingers at her belt.

Ne Chantez Pas Melencolie

Over level low barley his long
shadow moving, a taut root of old vine
in his hand, he comes walking.
There is his family, two heads.
Setting their picnic on stubble
between a low yellowing orb
and a tree. He marks this tree's
foliage ordered like ferns, knobbed
with green sorbs, which will brighten,
soften, and ochre on ochre fall
on hard earth.
                          Low light
lances the flat of their valley
sharply arranging toys down there
as a village, two miles away. Inside
the leaves of the sorb tree mistletoe
clumps show blacker green,
he observes. There is a nylon half
moon looking into the orange now
nearly comfortable heat of the sun.
Between the striped chairs,
on the picnic table ripe peaches,
variety *white*, and red wine.
He also observes how green grapes,
alongside walled boxes of barley,
hang bunched already.

   He lifts flushed arms to air.

He regards his girl and her mother,
he thinks (not so far off at Blois,
across this low ochre of fields,
after exile) of Charles d'Orléans'
sixties. *Chantez ce que vous
pensés*, this evening — yet,
Ah! que vous m'anuyés, Viellesse,
need it be, *de pis en pis*,
chantez Melencolie?

The Chapel

This being one of the days for me
When the word death tolls, I find
The chapel of O Spes Unica
I've driven to see is closed;

In which, on black touch, a poet
Of a poet says, "I was his friend."
For whatever reason, because a boy
Yesterday smashed off a staid

Effigy's alabaster toes, or because
Today the verger's dead or to his
Married daughter in Nottingham goes, I say
The chapel of O Spes Unica is closed.

No Sprinkling of Bright Weeds

Earth—that old-hat phrase of superseded days—
goes red with my slack-satin flowers,
my poppies; my cornflowers of absolute blue—
both mix into my wheat. Also out of the ears

with which it's level stares each sepal-criss-
crossed flat corncockle eye,
magenta, without a blink the whole
day into the hot sky.

   Lady, not now. Lady in whose gay
bleached hair with ears of wheat with poppies if not corn-
flowers and cockles mixed, and in your south love-
in-the-mist and black-pupilled scarlet pheasant's eye,

Sunburned Ceres, you must understand (you catch my
tone) that now across all plains—no longer fields—
your very carefully treated wheat must be
a clean stand for maximated yields.

Our bodily, of course our economic and our
     advertising needs
permit, Lady, except among peasants backward on thin
     soil,
no sprinkling of bright weeds.

Hill of the Bees

Under terracettes and bushes of steep slopes
are these: tracks, hollows, holes, maples, yews, most
muscular ash boles. Over streams are:
dips, slades, slacks,
ditches, mint nooks, hunt gates, springs, night.
Into these by old habit
and tenure we do project ourselves or portions
of us or what in degrees of our likeness we inherit.

At least we did; breathe then
they did back again: the whole companionage,
night, springs, hunt gates, mint nooks, slacks, slades,
ditches, dips, streams;
those muscular ash boles, yews, maples, holes, hollows,
tracks, bushes, terracettes, high slopes:
the lot—all that companionage.

That substantial instability, let it
wither and dry, let it—when, say,
night away from a too
great staring of night-killing light at least
in our words "seems breathing" — die,
or be unfelt, we die.
Unpicking the nest of most warm
feathers we have so long, soft if deluding,
from our own breasts, our own undercoverts torn.

A Myth Enacted

They form, these hill-holding uneven elms and limes,
A Hercules in great trouble, for our troubling times,
Lashed down by dwarfs, not resting at ease,
Unable at all, heave, thresh, as he may in a great Sept-
    ember wind,
To snap the dwarfs' fruit-net of fine strings.
Wind drops, his efforts cease, he has no strength,
Arrows of rain pelt on his prostrate length,
Great Dorset Hercules being no longer lifting thighs and
    knees
Has again collapsed to a soughing moaning rough run of
    trees.

Après La Chasse
In Memory of Maurice Beaubrun

Repent. Why? Not a kingdom of
heaven is at hand
where a for once clement king,
viz. otherwise a colonel, absolute,
will check, perhaps, if you do,
if you trust his promises,
his electric torturer's clean hand.

Repent. Yes, enough. But not
because you fear a punishment, or
being shut out. Too late for that.
Repent? Admit at least in pursuit
you went often too far.
Also, in the fairground in the distorting
true mirror hesitated to recognize

Sufficiently what you are,
who are not genius or saint also.
Repent, but not too much,
no grub by grub crawling in white. Old
friend, the kingdom, soviet, democracy—no,
the small mild hamlet of free
felicity, brief, is not of such.

Slow Bell from the High Hill

Childhood is over, all things end,
I no longer half hear my child with children
Playing below me in the half darkness
Of the hollow foreign lane
Where the dead tramp lay.

All things end—if even at first
Growing is an end: all things begin.
Of course, of course. But ends begin,
And with a never out of fashion
Slow bell from the high hill.

Models of Deity

Goddess of gold–streaked
hair and sweetest navel, naked,
how by white doves killed and slit
throats of kids
and bloodied fleeces
in—above blue sea—high places
aromatic,
could you have been
delighted, and placated?

Your question, late questioner,
is elementary,
and evasive. At least
in my time I was better
than most earlier—
and some later—
models of beastly deity
which you created.

André Bauchant's Mill
Under a Pink Rose

It happens I know who in this abandoned tan-mill
Lived, suffered, and knew being's exquisite delight,
Treading the causey over his loosestrife meadows,
Treading this black, plank bridge which crosses this black
    river,

To these hollow rooms, this great bread oven now damp
And always cold, this chimney by reversed irons braced;
To this black lane going up through woods of ash.
His mad wife screamed, and silver—all the more—this
    flat

Valley seemed, silver the nude ash stems, pure the pro-
    cession
Of small clouds; Roman chariots he imagined in these
    meadows,
Dancers in evening. Heavy with much grief his now
    abandoned
Hollow home, and with much loveliness, and leaving it

Down the firm straight raised lane in evening August
    light,
At the far end of which for me a figure waits, back
I look at the round rose of a startling cloud over his
    woods
Which are a long grave bar of green, or black, above his
    home.

Career of a Sharp-profiled Public Servant

He tied himself to four umbrellas
and jumped—admittedly it was not high—
from the E.E. tower of his father's church.

He rolled, feet together, hands tight to each side,
over primroses to the edge of the cliff on his father's
    glebe
and stopped—exactly—3 inches from

a fall of 200 feet. He was imprisoned
in the Russian Revolution, and came home
and to test that nerve

climbed to the top of the steel-framed
mile-measurer above that cliff, and stood there
as before, on one foot, in the high wind,

and he became, the manes of our house-master
will learn with relief, the most conventional
pimp of the Crown,

and was ennobled.

Fulke the Black

He lay in bed on holiday, a short grey man
Eyeing the blood-red roses on the ceiling paper,
Imagining he owned six donjons, a Fulke Nera
Who sent missives saying "Hang the bearer,"
A sweaty-bellied, hairy-penis'd,
Heartily laughing raper;
To whom there came *thé Éléphant,* two *brioches,*
And the morning paper.

St-Hilaire-de-Harcouet

The Just Inheritance

Yes, but I like it, on White Island on sea-
Campion leaning over the Atlantic staring
To water and air meeting. Why not?
Who is the worse because I like it?
Should it be the occasion of a sneer,
From me, or Alvarez, or recent history?
Very well, I hear too the black cow of the ocean
On her weed-rock moaning; if also
Some relief inherited I value.

Sad Grave of an Imperial Mongoose

Under this weeping ash or umbrella tree
protrudes among white and purple crocuses
the small tombstone of a mongoose
inscribed "Darling Riki-tiki. R.I.P."

He died because, when brought "home"
by a senior member of the Indian Civil Service
on his retirement he could not stand of course the cold
climate of this green vale. And now the Raj having gone,

the Civil Servant having gone (at one of the two uni-
versities
of the time he began with a first class degree in the
classical learning, largely, of a former empire), his child-
ren too
having gone (he—and they—were cremated and scattered,
but he has

an entry in *Who was Who*), the house as well having
changed hands
into other families, this stone among broken crocuses
over the small
ribs of Riki-tiki pierced a few inches down by threads
from
crocus corms and wandering rootlets of the umbrella tree

remains—other than the entry in *Who was Who* and a
short piece
imprisoned flatly in a huge back volume of *The Times*—
the sole
indication of the career of one who said
"Many of my best friends are Indians", also "Habeas
Corpus hardly

could apply to Indians"; as he administered justice
Socratic and Ciceronian under the aegis—a phrase
whose broad propriety he would have
understood—of, after all,

an uninspiriting empire. Though it is easy to look back.

John Hunter's Canal

Then as requested turning
round my leg, I caught
a particular name
in what the surgeon—

To his pair of student
doctors—said: it was
attached to some canal
by which the blood inside me

From my stitched thigh
fell: canal of that
grand Orion
of the rational

Sky, grand Hunter of out-
rageously extended bones
and bottled twins
and kidney stones

Who paid
Chardin for canvases
of the quiet grace
of man; and also set,

In London, Haydn
in his old age
humming out his *Twelfth
Night* canzonet.

  ★ ★ ★

It was a pleasure—
though there followed
an injected stinging
of some 5 c.c.—

To think this morning
of that bright Orion
of the human calling,
lover of cool

Harmony, injector
of himself—to see—with organisms
of V.D.,
commemorated, not below

Some periwig or Tory
briber's marble, but
—it flattered me—
inside my own anatomy.

Occasions of Bones

You put a small hand into the chest-tomb,
White chervil around, and found as if
They were a child's bricks wedged or large
Snails, together, unwoken, for winter glued,
Skulls. With skulls was the stone box crammed.

Well, you said, this is the country, different
From England, where living is only a stomping
Pause before being dead. Then our driver
Half round a hard hairpin stopped, grinned
And softly he said it was the point where in the crossness
He'd shot a Tan dead.

We rowed through a blue bay next day,
Skellig held a coif, blue mountains rose,
On a small island we came to land, where
Remnants of a chapel sprawled, the dead
Lay there in scraps as well, washed out
Surprisingly on to the sand. Did then

These white thin ribs and shins
Make us, more than that shock-headed, soon dead
Sallow poet of Ireland, think particularly
—I think not, dead one—on that occasion
Of the sinfulness
Of our own merry sins?

Language of Stairs

Language of stairs: I lie in bed,
You open letters, then you tap,
Tap up quick
On the hollow stairs:
It's something good,
Someone—but who?—
Is coming, or,
A cheque's arrived

(In honesty should I
Reverse these two?),
A book, for once
A not intolerable review.
The speed, lightness
Of taps I interpret knowing
By this stair-language when for us it's
Something pleasurably new.

If it is something else you learn
From opening letters,
You do not
Speak a hollow slow march
Up the stairs, or (I think) give
Way to tears. You go to typing, or the loo,
Having spread the letter by my plate,
For once glad I get up late.

Spleen Again of the Night Picnic

Now in violet the big round moon,
While soup is heated on the track
And blackberries
Fall into our hands:
Sunset-shining
Were the first we picked, the moon
An intimation only in the haze.

Now, in violet this big moon;
Now, stubble glinting; westward, Mars;
Now metal of our picnic table, not
This night air, cold.

They say,
They say, It is serene. But I am not a
Brother of Basho, senriu, not
Haiku, is my kind. I'm
Failed by the abstruse. I say,
It is a full moon rising
In a matt of violet only.
It is stubble only
Because of moonlight glinting, and only
Mars between
The sunset and the risen moon.

And under, somewhere, this great
Space wild cars klaxon
For the wed; and with a trail
A high plane
Underwrites the moon.
And I decay, and my illusions
Go. Grace, which is
Best, is not substantial,
Does not go on, is, against the cruel,
Not strong, recoils
From suffering.

Killing abhorred, the Panchen Lama
Hired Dark and Years to kill
At last the man, in a wet
Dungeon, whom
He could not kill.

Or Perhaps the Mystic Rose between the Legs

When out at night
I wish to express my wonder
Seeing a whole moon through white
Clouds in a great ring of amber

Past high leaves shining
Of a scented poplar,
God, I say My God,
What a bloody wonder.

I don't claim God in that exclaiming
Has atavistic merit:
It is a shell of a word
I happen to inherit.

Clumsily to that riding orb should
I exclaim "All Men Who've Been"?
Well, if I take to bits My God,
It is that I mean.

White Tom's Position

Tom, Tom, the pedants' father,
Master of perhaps and rather.

Join your fingers, cross your knees,
Tell young poets to say please.

From your perch in Russell Square
Teach duchesses the art of prayer.

Teach the Tories to discount
Your master's Sermon on the Mount.

Teach the flaccid is the sound,
Proclaim the Pegasus of Pound.

Gird at Lawrence, Hardy, Blake,
For the Church of England's sake—

    etc., and soon

        Over the Missouri, over the Seine,
           Over the Thames, and over the Severn,
        The soul of white Tom
          Shall float to Heaven.

Note for a Genealogical Tree

My father dying well past eighty
Spoke almost in coma of a girl
He loved when he was twenty.

Theology was his reading then.
"I say nothing of my reading," so his student's
Diary went, "it was theology,"

And he was soon ordained, and so (I think)
His wilder being mostly
Was contained.

Her home was Ventnor, things
About this girl from Ventnor (he sent
Her roses) from his diary he erased.

My mother—what did she dream of, young?
Old, in her drawing-room, filling her armchair,
By a February fire,

She slept. Her last son's young
Wife sighed, she heard, she snapped
"Ridiculous!" and slept.

107

Paddington Street

By the low gas fire which sent
Its red suffusion through the room
I undressed you; to your sweet
Navel bare, and small, exquisitely
Shaped you were.
Yet in that dry warm unharsh gloom
You reached over (horizontally)
And took the phone. You rang
Your husband, and you said,
I shall not be home. And, I am not alone.
I loved you. But what hating
Made you, over me, your breast
Touching my own, most graceful
One, reach to the phone?

A Dozen Facts of London

Innumerable bodies in clothes mell along the veins of our
city. Here are joints, in a side-vein, where money is paid
to see bodies removing clothes, and then not shaking
invisible quims. This cannot be transferred to beetles.
Cats do not understand. Micro–organisms are too busy
spreading as always into tracts for living. The booted
Black Guards and the Pigs off duty keep to their seats,
not even handling their tucked away cocks. The play
proceeds.

I have been on the beaches of the filthy Thames, and have
found a brown domino, a three and a two, of mutton
bone, stuck in grey slime between the pebbles.

A bald crone sells smoked fish in Brewer Street. It might
be the phloem of a soft tree she slices from the back of a
sturgeon. Bright herrings know nothing of their
posthumous existence here rolled up in glazed shallow
bowls of immense circumference.

Words at the head of my dictionary. I look for a spelling. I am intrigued on the way, and have found out the pomeloe, which is "a variety of the shaddock"; and just before that the polatouche, which is "a Siberian flying squirrel."

On my way I know a Paradise. In this Paradise there are no primeval parents, and no formal hunters. Above it the sky is poured coolly into position from five pallid towers of suavely insubstantial concrete. Intersecting railway lines enclose a triangle: this is my inaccessible Paradise. It contains rank shrubs, long grasses; and beasts which are not hunted, and protestant old Cranach painting them. And me, over Cranach's shoulder watching them.

Ahasuerus is to be observed climbing mountains: the lower ramps incline gently from Charing Cross Road and St James's Square and the Yard at Havard. Ahasuerus climbs slowly, he sees no one but a reflection of himself, he sees occasionally a Glory around the shadow of his head on mist below him. He has read Coleridge. He looks up to the next hold for his pudgy hand. He climbs, yet vertigo and the chance of falling are his pleasures. He has cut his beard short, vertical sunshine blisters his neck below his ginger hair. He has climbed out of sight.

On my way, the pathos of a literary party. I wait for my companion, to go up in the wheezy lift. In New York it might be a pert lift. I wait and I observe The First Cabinet of Mr Gladstone. The party is promoted by a newspaper. The elderly recognize each other and talk of when they were young. The young are timid. The literary editor hands a cheque equivalent to the salary earned in a month by a police inspector or by a whore in a week to a she novelist who has written the five millionth novel since the first novel was written in English. What he says, what she says, nobody hears. What she has written, few at the party will read. The elderly talk of when they were young, the young are timid. Most in the room do not know each other's identity; or their own.

The pathos of a literary party. It is given, by his publisher, to honour the poet in the corner; standing in his coffin in the corner, protruding his head into the noisy room. This cadaver protrudes further into the noise a strong jaw, pitted and green. The jaw moves, but if this cadaver speaks I hear nothing. Are his poems good? Are we privileged? Is this an occasion which will be recorded in memoirs, or a journal? Did you write that review of my father's poems? Has this corpse a son who will be a publisher and will ask such a surly question in Boston, or Chicago?

Once, before all such were sent under cover, it was possible to see in every doorway along Brewer Street the blond aureoles of prostitutes shining in evening sunlight. It was as if angels by an early master stood in sunshine in diminishing perspective along a forest avenue in Savernake, obscene mushrooms pure among the leaves.

The acids of naming and of time which loosen structure and corrupt the surface, permit the grasp of the affections. They do not attack these blocks of offices, number by number, which are blocks and do not rise to a tower looped by the unlikely rosiness of the morning or the more orange and comforting red of the evening. A tight arse (which did emerge from a womb) superintends the transfer of money in bags from hands I saw briefly in the opening of a security car, as if they were the hands of a Lazarus who declined to rise. A drawer in the basement is full of the dried skins of the polatouche, which is "the flying squirrel of Siberia", and this drawer is labelled in Cyrillic characters.

Here I note on my way eidetic visions in colours stood up in front of a poet. And here the nature of the incidence of cholera was observed from the loose dead, who had drawn from a single pump.

Along all of the squalid street under breaking buildings green avocadoes glitter in boxes. Polished fruits of bald heads of old salesmen, brown coconut heads of the whiskered. Fog at the cross-streets changes from red to green.

110

When Finally

What shall we Stoics do
When, finally, we're faced
  With going under?

Pressing on the rounded
Flap of each ear won't
  Suppress that thunder.

A call on God—at last—
Will not at all
  Fight off our panic,

When the rafts have left
Us on the high impossible hills of
  Our *Titanic*

OK, OK,
Again repeats our motions,
  By long habit;

Myxamatosed, each man
Of us into a bulge-
  Eyed rabbit

        ★   ★   ★

Bombs fell, the pale
Citizenry ran and lied how
  They could take it;

Like whom, the most we
Most of us can do
  Is fake it.

Expulsion

Driving them out,
Flapping from flowering tree to tree,
He manages his great blade's vicious
Fire as smartly as he can.

He was no good
Angel who did this to man.

As Dufy Paints

Wise Coleridge says the happy poem is the best,
And English poets write of sadness best, or most.
There is, I do regret, our rhyming three
Sad, mad and bad: which do succeed the glad.
But, to be sure, as Raoul Dufy paints,
To write like the bright sap green
Which lights dry saddening banks
Beside charcoal of hard roads in the spring
(Adding rose madder and a deep sky blue)
For all of us is good; and is for the sadder
Writers, a most enviable thing.

The White Doves

They rose out of dead men,
out of their mouths,
gently, white doves,
to branches where they fidgeted
at first a little,—
free, uncertainly.

It was something,
white doves for the souls of men,
instead of the roving idiots

112

of the morning, cuckoos,
or jackdaws cackling or identical
factory chickens chelping, or worse.

White doves
even the souls of the worst.

Picture of a Saturnine Profile

As if in a picture by an unknown master
I see a bald priest long-nosed, goat-faced,
Delineated over me in the unevennesses of the plaster.
He kneels, of course; his vestments encircle half his head.
I think he prays for the repose, which he thinks not
Likely to be granted, of an evil grandee at last dead;
Or he meditates on the stinking nature of man
Or of God rather by whose great guilt he supposes
Began our guilty and peculiar tribe of man.

My last half-hour in bed so invaded,
On a morning of late snow I write this down,
Look up, light has changed and my saturnine
Priest has faded.

The Cyprian's Spring

The Cyprian's Spring by water only can be
reached, your pedalo moored to a hole in rock
on the slight slap of violet water. Press
your right shoulder to tearing rock along
a narrow path, brush the magenta
of wild gladioli, enter shadow, before which
also pomegranates flower. Swallows fly out,
the Cyprian's Spring breaks out, so many bright
gallons per cool minute, so many bright
gallons per cool hour, so many gallons

per cool century, so many glittering gallons
per cool aeon.

Swallows fly in, fly out,
in wild figs overhead are doves. Wet ferns
of black filaments slenderer
than the Cyprian's secret hair move
in the water breeze.

Come here alone,
there is no room for two.

Back in the arrogant
sun, if you upset your pedalo, and tumble
in, expect sharp stinging of purplish-black
sea-urchin spines.

The Gods and the Colonels

If one saw an actual snake
wreathing through an actual
skull's eye.

Instead I arrange such a tableau
with a rubber viper and a badger's skull
and have left it on the spare
room window sill.

And somewhere cold
clear water flows under
pink oleanders of
Theocritus—

whom I should, I think, now
spell Theokritos, de novo,
judge of the gods, accent
on the i—

without
cutting of the throat
of a white kid. But

the gods and the colonels
whom they serve, the whole
time insist
on blood.

Tame Life Park

A duke, his bowlered daughter, a tenant,
     A scarlet-veined
  Arselicker, and a squire,
Look out expectantly on Saturday morning,
  From the wrong side of the wire.

On the Foxes, who spend their Saturday morning
  Poking lumps of sugar through the wire,
At a duke, his bowlered daughter, a tenant,
     A scarlet-veined
    Arselicker, and a squire.

Wild Life Park

Flutters the fuckgale, standgale,
Galefucker (yes, names for him respectable
Dictionaries   actually   enshrine)—kestrel,   windhover,
  kingdom
Of daylight's dauphin in his a little-dappled-flattened
Clinging to meshes of fine wire.

Trails from his left claw a chick: more such
Pus-yellow fluffs or powder-puffs of dead
Chicks from a farm
Sag under these wired-in naked branches dropped
By these half-dozen tedium's dauphins on this
Wet staleness of their ground.

A stink of fox, from curled foxes
Asleep on quarry ledges in the next cage,
Sneaks round.

Sequence in East Cornwall

i   Lansallos

Wet liverwort, wet rock.

Thread of a fall, and
spray;
joggling on stones until
the kettle's filled.

Mint is trodden. Wild madder
clings. Bartsia above, stiff,
shaking, the wind there brisk.

Then the small
stranded whale at an angle
just alive,
on the shelving beach,
its wide flukes convulsing.

ii   Talland Sands

Fennel, smelt off your fingers:
is the tide out?
Then the Japanese bridge,
gap in the hedge, and red
bars of rock.

I kiss you, a flush
comes up your neck as red
as these smooth rocks.

I lose my nerve, and clothes
of others lie on the red rocks:
so we move on to
liquid ghosts of shrimps
in shallower pools.

iii   Off Polperro

It is the sun rising—I do not recognize it and I am
ribbed about it—out of the heavy
channel under which,
under us, under our stinking smack,
spreads the toponymy of rocks,
invisible, named rocks, named
ledges, hollows, named in extinct
Cornish, visited by the drowned
only, all the same familiar as
potato plots cut among matted
bent blackthorn along cliffs, to
fishers, out of Peter's porth or pool.

For centuries known;
at any rate before
they drank at fishing dawn
black thick sweet tea
from chipped enamelled rusted mugs.

iv   Longcoombe

Three steps in rock

under an ivied
oak leaning outwards
holding
in an old stick nest
dirty round
eggs of an owl.

But to you I attend,
not to the owl's eggs or
to whatever

117

home or mill has left
these bereft
worn steps

in wood-saged rock.

v   West Looe River

My darling, half-
naked among noisy flaked
leaves of cinnamon
off pearled beeches
high over a curl of the high
tide river.

Earlier it was among
bluebells, broken.

vi   Trelawne Mill

On the white plaster of the ruined cottage
you draw in two colours a goddess.
Now is it night. You have woken, by
candlelight in which you gleam,
you hunt hopping fleas
over the taut sheet, with a dampened
thin end of soap.

Hosh whimpers, wrinkled, in a dream.

It is day nearly. I have no doubt
of shining peal slipping
through the pools, upstream.

vii   Coldrennick

Upstream: rare osmundas, mundic
and silver ore. Downstream a bog myrtle

118

thicket. In between, wet
moss-dome of a dipper's
nest below the bridge from which we
lean, we see foreshortened
the anyhow short
bird of white and black
move through the clear if
rippled stream.

Hold my cold hand.

viii   Botelet

Realization of emotions
as mimulus, yolks of eggs, lucid,
broken all along this stream:

so now I reject
the grey pampas plumes,
dry, snapped,

beyond the fastigiate
yews and the iron gate to our
cemetery, creaking.

Who lies there
is not you.

Cotswold Country

Her papa belonged to the Art Workers' Guild,
It was with Beauty he was filled,
In the Cotswolds he didn't care
If all the Jews were killed.

It comes of that: she pins the skull of a bat
Mounted in gold in her hat.
She hangs Concrete poems up in a mill,
And her breasts are flat, and it all comes of that.

Celebration

Celebrate we the Great Nothing

Led by Coifi, Archpriest, in glorious vestment,
And by our long-nosed, horse-toothed
Archminister, in simple undress,
And by our Mayor in chain,
And by our Chief Lead Soldier,
And by our Head of the Humanist Association
Powdered with talcum,
And by our Poet of the Moment,
And by our white-haired Television
Star, masturbating, who is Renegue,
But calls himself Repentance,
And last by our Unknown Warrior,
In a new, but inexpensive suit,
Who is causing members of this distinguished
Company, as at the raising of Lazarus,
To pinch their nostrils.

Celebrate we the Great Nothing. But oh,
Celebrate we the Celebration.

        Two minutes silence.

(N.B. The Royal Female Principle is away
Having her infertile womb scraped by the chief
Of her Royal College of Obstructions)

        The guns boom.

There are no doves. Only absurd pelicans squawk,
Flapping their clipped and yellowed wings.

About the Isle of Man

*(for Archbishops and Cardinals, and Headmasters at
Prayers, and Brigadiers at Church-parade, and the Queen)*

Since he began,
Man has thought—not surprisingly I'd say—
There's a Mystery about Man.
Who must be explained, and sustained, by a Plan,
By the G plan for Gods,
Or by the X plan for Odin up on a cross
Or Christ also aloft,
Or by the Y plan.
Particularly by the Y plan
(Or to judge by the favourite
fantasy-reading at present of Man it could be
he was made for a Spy plan).

I'm not sure it's the worse for Man
If for the first time since he began
He begins to realize there's been
No Plan for Man,
Who must now, Poor Man,
Do as they do on the Isle of Man,
Which is — What they can.

Through Butterflies

Not requiring to look into many faces,
    into yours only.
Not requiring to ask where that road goes.
    It goes.
I know its destination, I have no map only of
    its intervening track
Through dandelion grasses, then
    rippling of fords,
Climbing to a dry karst slowly; through
    butterflies, past
Debris of picnics, stones of the executed,
    and through junipers.

121

Plane Tree in a Château Garden

Every minute or so from the grand tree something des-
cends.
Excrement of an insect tumbles, a leaf clatters, a scale
Of the grey bark drops off, revealing, if I could see, a
yellow.
Also I watch leaves turn, leaves
Shiver, which hang at the end of branches which are not
moved,
Which are zigzags high up.
                                        I watch a white parachute
Seed of a minor plant: it floats, expedition
Of continuance losing hardly an inch of height
Through the space vaulted in a big way by these leaved,
Dividing zigzags. It crosses, and it floats
From view: I raise two hands and coldness
Of the stone bench in this great heat comes into me.

  Now I resent
Twinkles of sunlight which enter and interrupt,
And destroying voices, which come nearer.
My two hands raised, I know I should know this
Grand trunk, this grand branched vault impending.

Château de Poncé

Water Voice of a Dove

Resting in great heat by running water,
Yes, under a waving willow
By water we have called, viz. chuckling,
Prattling, chattering, I heard how a dove's
Voice is a voice of water, floating
On the voice of water, like the voice
Of passing water staying. So
I slept.

122

To Dijon, under Snow

Tomorrow I fly to Dijon, and today
Looking at the Master of Moulins'
Painting, at that baby in a Burgundy stable
Under his blue-dressed mother's
Thin astounded fingers,
Chancellor Roland kneeling, his fat dog
On his red robe, Burgundian shepherds
Watching from the green, I say,
As we say innumerably, *If*
This was so, If this was so,
If so ordinary a thing as a birth
Was so beyond all ordinary births,
If from the ordinary arose that extraordinariness
By which all was pardoned, all absolved,
Resolved. If just a little
Of this worked so—

And know that, holding us, a descendant, not
Discordant myth must grow.

The Cold Spring

Traveller, don't drink the sun-warmed water
Of this beck my trailing sheep have muddied so,
But climb the hill there where the heifers graze,
And go a few yards on, and you will find below
That shepherds' pine, bubbling from wet rock,
A spring colder than northern snow.

From the Greek of Leonidas

Note on the Untraditional

Lord, My God, Your Temple, his poems begin:
Differently others, including your humble,
Who are less avid of sin,
Repeat his ecstatic reverse of a grumble;

In which I consider he spoke
Of renewal of singing—it happens—by commonplace
    birds,
Of light down, golden section, hard structure, texture,
Sparkle, single and multiple curves.

These he left out, but I say his descendants
Have learnt it is far from a screaming sin
To leave out God and in grace
To put the facts in.

Desultory Summer Poem

i

It is a luxury, so circumstanced in summer,
Thinking of affection as abstraction,
Separate from you.

Clouds
Out of the huge cloud-gulf of the west
Come up, ferns of asparagus
Across them wave. One cloud
Passes, releases cool wind along my
Upper arm, then
Sting of the sharp sun.
A blue smoke rises from a yard below,
Thins to a less blue, and through
The mucked horizon of near trees a paling
Threads a close-set pattern down.

I scratch the bites across my wrist,
Hear leaves, observe blue smoke now
Against grey of a fat cloud re-
covering the sun; I think, I say,
Of this abstract of affection (you
Having gone to town) and, in
Some photo, of round Ionesco's
Face of a clown unbrutishly repeating
All's absurd.

ii

My habits are not regular, I don't
Set periods aside or work by a clock.
I should do nothing oftener, think
Of you more and of affection
Less, eyeing always that
Which is automatic.

I think, when she interrupted,
I should have given just now the slim
Gypsy child the two coins she
Held out her hand for. Some moments
Reveal too much and—just as well—
Are deliberately, quickly forgotten:
I was too lazy, I accepted
The estimate of gypsies,
Which may be correct; stopping the luxury
Of thinking of affection,
I should have gone indoors and fetched her
The money she asked for—Why not?
I acted
Like that balding Fool in London who's
Collected a Council of Fools to consider
Not their prurience but what they
Suppose obscene: the child followed
Her *métier,* I was stingy, I followed mine,
And it rains now and I am forced
Away from the sibilance of the sad bullfinches
In deep leaves behind me:
I should remember longer than I shall

125

That I was mean (not only because that
Child-gypsy was naked-footed
And was slim).

iii

In the sky scene as I move I notice
The greyness of the underside of the great
Cloud now above me; and a round
Hole through this grey, and in this hole
Blue, and the white
Top of a thunder-cloud unseen otherwise away
In the queue of the clouds.
By this is excused nothing,
Illuminated nothing, symbolized
Nothing—unless accident, accident,
Can be described as something?
Such as myself or you? Such as the gypsy
Child, such as that noble ninny in London
(Whom I recall as a petulant
Blond-haired undergraduate tossing
His wonder mop when he was found
Out in one more pious intellectual stupidity)?

   It is raining heavily. I shall
Continue, indoors, reading
Of the severer absurdity
Of the Archpriest Avvakum, adjuring
His Old Believers to stride into the flames
And fix themselves to the stake. "For this
We came out of our mother's womb. You
Will not be long burning. A twinkling
Of an eye, and the Soul is free."
The Soul.

   It strikes midday through the rain,
From the church above, for the second time.
I hear the burr of the car
With you returning.

126

A Pause on High Downs, in a High Wind, after Buying Pignotti's Giorgione

Angels, protrude your long thin trumpets glistening
Out far from your black shelf of cloud:
Greet, angels, with tender voluntaries of your perfection
The minute soul flying through vast freedom upwards,
Having left behind its sagged body in a shroud.

O if this could be so, I exclaim.
But to perfection
Have we imagined it. In such perfectness have
As well fresh trees against light, in light
Been painted. So much must be allowed.

The Lawn of Trees and Rocks

It was on the flat of a valley, where for some cause trees
   stood back—
Trees had not been shuddered then by the heavy flint or
   the heavy gabbro axe—
Sunlight (between gold and diamond, hot and cool) il-
   luminated
At a morning angle a most green sward,
Nearly bisected, narrowly, by a stream. This rippled, but
   never hid
The pieces of red quartz which were its descending
   slightly winding bed.

It was here they grazed, their movement provoked a
   scent
Of mint. The barbarian hominid concealed in leaves could
Not detect their hooves, but heard the tearing of their
Plentiful food: bull, cows, heifers, calves, Bos primi-
   genius
Who would be painted inside caves, grazed
In this medium sun, and flicked a tail, moved,
And only seldom raised a head.

Homunculus

Beastly you are, wonderful,
tough, vulnerable,
damp Admirable, just out
of your black cocoon.

Enfolding you, I wonder
what name to give
to a book about
the world you are in, the young

leaf which holds you.

Fictional View on the Equator

Damp heat in God knows what tropical
Eyot of abandoned empire
Under the huge leaves, sagging, of an undeciduous tree
A narrow man with ulcers repellent, who is, who was,
He seldom recollects, a Ph.D.,
His fat woman using her black thumb for digging
Jiggers out of the brown bosom resting on her knee,
And that novelist, that fallen angel, G.Greene,
(See *Macbeth IV, 3*) watches from the sick leaves
Of another poisonous hairy-fruited tree.

It is a common language which this climate speaks
Translatable from such excess humidity—
Ay me, ay me, soe much I sigh to see—
Into dry temperate terms
Of living graciously.

A Comment on Buttercups
and the Reply of a Dwarf Who Lives in a Hole
behind the Conservative Club

Hell to these accustomed English buttercups
Of this bowl of dressed salad stuff
In which we live,
And to these blunt
Horse Chestnuts

Heaving in as usual June
5,000,000 flowers by gardens, open,
To prove owners
Better heeled than some. I say: "Dwarf,
Cut me a new rune."

"Revealing—if it can be read,"
You from your hole sneer, "Just what? except
The last invariability
(It's vanity, your flag of red)
Of being dead."

If Wearing My Old Goat's Skin

If wearing my old goat's skin down Reviewers' Lane
I cried the birth of a Byron or a Blake again,
Who would look out, or even hear,
Or give up buggering his bald Teddy-bear?

Bluebottle

I shall not kill that spiralling bluebottle
with my poisoned aerosol. His wings
cut a genuinely charming murmur of
all past good summers through the room,

again, and again. If this present
good summer was done with, and he walked out
from underneath my papers and on his feet went
slowly and fatly round,
he'd be unfortunate.

Thought on Fudge and Crystal

There are many ways of making fudge,
The cubic products are all much the same,
In litteris
Fudging is what fudgers do
And fudge is the generic name.

In which physics of the word
Crystal is to be preferred.

Burial in September

The old ones go to each other's funerals,
The old ones mourn themselves.
It is sometimes in perfection of the weather
In, as now, the ending summer
When shoe-darkening wetness of the grass of lawns,
And graveyards, does not dry or dull
Until about the tolling of the bell.
Not even the cleric thinks of heaven,
No one who's here has visions of a hell.
Glad that it's over, sons go off to their gravid
Wives or to their girls. And driving
Home slowly, in their expensive limousines,
The old ones mourn themselves.

Entente Cordiale
for the Common Market

O happy land where senators evade
The taxes by the vicious workers paid,
Where, like the courtyard gravel from the pits,
The newly born are graded and their futures fixed,
Where painted wells are built from worn-out tyres
And prefects are corrupted liars
Who boast and boast of scintillating glory
Invisible in the national story;
Where guiltless effluents foul each river
And brutal marc breaks down at last the liver,
Where rusting shacks defile the sand
All along the glittering Biscay land;
Where art can get no dole from trade
And meanness rules, so frescoes fade
And oak saints on their altars crumble
And medieval donjons likewise tumble—
Land of Algerian wines, and Catholic trance,
My three times happy, three times fertile France
Whose genial *yes* enamels Fascist *no*,
Whose stunted infants only fail to grow,
Many are the reasons why I love you so.

Aet Beran Byrg

Tired from being, unfresh plants are dying,
A scent of matted nettles
Makes an atmosphere.

I recall, there was a battle here,
A thousand—that means many—sprawling, kites,
Crows, a scent of dying.

Blood and disembowelling in the still dry
Autumn of campaigning. Defeat, fear, being caught
In the early dying

Light, or if escape,
Complaining, not any
Hopes at all remaining.

Two a.m.

Distant, clear, down low,
Are lights of men.
From on top of the greater lateral hills
The automatic revolving lighthouse of the oceanic
Island throws—and beyond doubts of
Warning and of safety—a far
Question, question into emptiness.

And all emptiness, all gravity,
Ultimacy, nothingness, are then
By us felt and seen. And we
Are small, instant, here.
And time is all round and all
Elsewhere; of which one other island now strikes
Two a.m. in the night somewhere.

Two hours more, then over
Sierras, monadnocks, lakes, prairies, taiga, ice,
Cays whitened by noddies, seas and seas and soiled
Tarred shingles, lightens a huge sky-
Arch, geranium-red, partly, so that we,
Spiders, blue neon flies, gay birds,
Etcetera, etcetera, in sun, are small, instant, here.

At least now, with our bodies close,
Be comforted.

Young and Old

You are young, you two, in loving:
Why should you wonder what endearments
Old whisper still to old in bed,
Or what the one left will say and say,
Aloud, when nobody overhears, to the one
Who irremediably is dead?

Monsieur Colin's Paint-box Garden

This July are few famous flowers
In Monsieur Colin's garden,
He died in the cold and rain.

And Madame Colin will not go into
Monsieur Colin's garden.
The green weeds are there again.

The first for fifty years
In Monsieur Colin's garden,
And they need little rain.

Dry flowers are choked by them
In Monsieur Colin's garden,
Savages camped there again.

Madame Colin will not look back
At Monsieur Colin's garden
When she leaves finally in November's rain.

And next will go up tall swings
In Monsieur Colin's garden,
Children running, savages turned out again.

To Wystan Auden

They said, Have you heard the news?
Serious they looked, were grey, and I guessed
Someone they and I held in affection
Was dead. Then they said, Auden is dead,
Then they said it was you.
They had caught a flash of your death
On the air. Out of doors was it cold
Ending of English September, soon
To be frozen. Tobacco flowers lagged and sweet
Peas waved on their shoulder. You were dead.
Later I waited. I heard an announcer say
We must catch up with the weekend news, and there
Sure were you, there flashed on your big
   Wrinkled phiz. But O
It was still, still as now must you
Always be seen. You were held there a second,
And O you had died in a second, without
Being ill as you feared.

Forty years now
Have slipped by since for some who were young
You became living's healer, loving's
Magician, for all of these years
The imposer of blessings.
You were our fixture, our rhythm,
Speaker, bestower, of love for us all
And forgiving, not of condemning, extending
To all who would read or would hear
Your endowment of words. There was a time—
I recall—when you were not. Once more
You are not. But time, after you, by you
Is different by your defiance.
In Vienna dead on a day
When the displaced by violence out
On the airport were practising violence,
When at home a mad politician prophesied
Violence, enjoying dismay. But this morning
Is different, my dear one. As well as

Your words are you here who will address
Us and bless us more, and no more.
In death you are living, and this
Is not the end of a day.

An Autumnal

Because gunmen kill hostages in banks,
Because gunmen are gunmen and
Because police torturers are police torturers
On account of their genes and their mothers,
Because there are massacres,
Am I not to say that I love you?

Who is helped if I refuse to say
There now are yellow leaves, sky-blue
Morning Glories and this
Morning-Glory-blue sky above you,
Or if I decline to admit
That tendernesses glove you?

With Loving and with Women

To be obsessed with loving and with women—
Well, why not? It is obsession with
Impossible completion, and with benediction.
Da nobis pacem—but with that peace, as well
Exhilaration.

Under Alkanet

Not quite still or too fierce that sharp
Cypress air, and not more than lightly
Or slightly thinking, either one of us then, of
What had nested certainly there,

135

You lay in the shadowed stone coffin;
Under blue alkanet, your bright
Head in the socket, between breasts your two palms,
Parodied death and prayer.

Steps crushed the gravel. Quickly upright,
And confused, you dusted dead
Leaves from your skirt, and shook
Death from your hair.

This Year the Dove

A sub July. Inside our hedge this year
Does the chilled
Dove not play
Incessantly her throat.

I see not one unconcerned dove
On the road; which then lifts, with no
Alarm, to a wire. Days heavily
If damply heated these presences

Prefer; in such from a depth coolly
Do they send their
Monotonous
Unmonotonous note

In the Crypt at Bourges, the Effigy of Jean Duc de Berry

You rest, your neat slippers rest
On your fast asleep bear in this
Crypt down here where they tomb every
Straw-seated grey broken chair.

136

Risbec, Meurice, hundreds more
Have incised their names up
And down in the soft grey
Polished stone of your gown.

Your eyes too are closed like
Your bear's, your mouth at last
Is turned down, the tip of
Your snub nose has gone.

Grey. Down here, alabaster duke, is
Not one gay coloured item of day,
Grey have become your tender rich
Hours, without flowers.

Metre of Recent Living

In our metre

> Bells are rung,
> Our river fills with Tide,
> Our middle of the morning
> Train rolls down,
> Little foxes
> Cross the ride
> Where their great-great-
> Grandmas died.
> Choirboys frilled
> Like peach-fed hams.
> Dirty-minded little rams,
> Every weekend
> Trill to Heaven,
> And in his flat
> Magnificat
> Our Left Foot
> Sings to grander
> Bevan.
> On *The Times*
> Now summer's come,

We flea the cat
Upon the page which
Features Levin.
Aimless cabbage-
Whites arrive,
The founder's silly
Lecture's given.
Marked by earrings
Thighs declare
Lady poets too
Are queer.
Impudic fungi
Smell like sin.
Seville oranges are in.
Various Pakenhams
Thick as rooks
Now bring out
Their autumn books,
And stand, but not
Like Ruth forlorn,
Among the stubbles
Of the porn.
Black rolls the smoke
From dawn to dawn.

So this year
Our measure goes
Not quite as sweetly
As a rose
Yet not exactly
Flat as prose.

Visit, and Variation without Guilt

When I lean my head back on my hands
And Vega is up there still above my nose
And hoarse young owls who have not learned
Their flutes are calling, and I expect
Another Leonid to be falling,

Candles light these talkers up, who break
Their peaches into two. He's cotton close on top,
She's coiled red hair, her Turkish
Earrings sway, she's aged; she is tired, having
Driven from the boat all day.

I think I hear her say
"Don't you agree?" Without words I say
"We're on the Earth, the two of you
And me," and thanks, without guilt, for this cooled
Earth, and them, flow out of me.

I don't notice what they say, they are
Friends, who have made a long detour. Before
Heat tomorrow creates another
Shrivelling midday deeper into decline of life
They will have driven away.

Autumnal

"Spectacles on my nose and autumn in my heart" — I. Babel

I suppose it wouldn't do—I mean it—to express that way
what used to be expressed by saying that the
leaves are falling.

Leaves aren't in every cognizance but all the same it's
really true that everywhere at least inside
the Northern Hemisphere the
leaves are falling.

There is a story of two maiden sisters in an upper flat
who could think only of a drift of leaves inside a
London (East End) park for
burying their cat.

They weren't much cognizant of leaves, but having had
   that
business with their cat, I think they'd take my meaning,
now I mention that once more the
leaves are falling.

And there's a critic for whom the interesting life
in literature is always black; for him leaves were not,
are not, never will be leaves at least on
trees, so never, never
can be falling.

But—though they're appalling—I cannot bother with
that rotten critic or that putrefying cat: with no
finality, without a supercilious that's that, I only mention
to myself—it's true, it's autumn almost, and
it's nothing new—all day, all day the altered
leaves are falling.

Another June

Let's think of June, which corresponds
To twenty-eight in women.

Petals of clumped peonies, it's true,
Have started falling.

But holidaying ants, and humans, so far
Are not swarming,

Winds are not driving, clouds are not
Blackly storming.

Even nights, as well as days, at last
Are positively warming.

To mutter "June is bluff" must be
Considered boring.

Were you asleep to all this summer stuff,
You would be snoring.

What we suppose repetitive may
Set us yawning.

But what else than Now is deity,
And worth adoring?

Note for Examiners

Late were Yeats and Tennyson
Virgins. Then as if all his years
Were lost and only nature left,
Into old age silver Tennyson
Wrote splendidly of sadness,
But ripe Yeats wrote in fury
Of defiant madness.

L'Ile Verte
(Site Classée. Camping Interdite)

Describe this celebrated site to me. Well,
First it is the clouds I see as rosy as small roses
Which are enclosing now a paring of a moon.
I see the yellowing *vert* of very slender trees

Aspiring past these rosy clouds to blue
(Of course, this setting shining paring
Of a moon is new). The clucking
Mobilettes have crossed, at last, the chattering

Bridge of wood, and they have vanished
Cheerfully through the lea, leaving this
River scene, tender like the young on mobilettes,
To all the scattered paper and to me.

Quelle Histoire

Light noises from slight birds
In trees which have not leaves,
And through white sunshine waftings
Of now warmer, warmer air. Each

Season I arrive it seems that dying
Momentarily recedes. The mercury
Stays up. I'm told, I soon forget, who
Went earlier in the coldness of the year.

This time—the mercury pushes higher—
It was, for one, Bertin *menuisier*:
In hospital one week he had no visit
From his wife. And he remembered in his bed

His young first wife, whose death
Of TB, at eighteen, he said,
Had cheated him of life (a baggy, dirty,
Tough grub was his second wife).

Now they would have cured her of TB,
Large Bertin said and said;
Who knew, O yes, that he was dying.
Of oak so many times he had made

A happy bed: in his iron dying
Bed—the mercury goes higher—only about
This loved first girl was large dull Bertin
Talkative, and silent, and then sighing.

A Matter of James (and Conrad)

I read of this man with despair.
I despair that after all I live elsewhere.
"Artist to artist talks": all I can do
Is read of this man with despair.

He read the other (he said so) like music rare,
Equal to equal, yet the circle with the square,
Surrendering to him to the deepest depth
He knew the good of him he could but fear.

"Art makes life": the artist's life is only there.
Deep was his life, restrained, austere;
Art being the harshest life to live of all
I read of this man with despair.

Unposted Reply

Of bright energy renewed slowly every
Bright morning less we retain. No more
Enough to make illumination fully
Again and again below unpromising rain.

Yet you have been, your letter says,
With your Especial Friend, in
Wharfedale in the rain laughing,
In a sports car, drawing bridges,

Seeing grey with mauve and with deep
Green a brown, object
Of you and Wharfedale and of rain.
Never, unless I prod you,

Do you say that you are old.
And I lament, and I should write
Content instead of this a shape
Like one you draw, or such

A plateau as you carve,
An Object, green with brown,
Which may be carried and unpacked, exhibiting
Your joy, in Rome, or Bonn.

The Bell

It was hair-raising,
A bereft woman's single
Moan, which I suddenly
Heard rising from down deep
Nearly to a yell

Behind elms greening. Birds
Called, lilacs were scent, coupled
Two black and scarlet
Beetles across sand. And I
Waited for the bell.

One Surface of Loving

How is it I have not celebrated
Your under-arm, from your wrist
To your elbow?

It is one of your
Gentlest surfaces, and at this moment
It lies on my cheek.

I have only to turn my head
Very slightly and my lips are
Against this surface of loving,

But you remove your arm from me
And instead you are now
Stroking my head.

Angles and Circles

Have I the "Spirit of Orthodoxy"?
I have not. But have I
The spirit of opposing? Perhaps—

I remember my mother complaining
"Criticize when you have a home
Of your own, if you ever have one."

And I "believe in Utopia"?
No. But it is a proper idea,
Utopia. It is proper to hope.

That "things may be better", for instance,
And go on being better. It is proper
Not to piss our corrosion over

The beds of the flowers. If miracles will
Not occur, there should be
Mutations; not that I fancy

Either Christ with a pistol (he used,
I reflect, to turn us over,
Naked, to demons) or Big Shots

Whose nature and actions are mercy.
For my neck not the stiff collar
Of the Men of State, or of God,

And not that soft collar God's Men
Affect when they ape us
In a bonhomous mufti,

And not the kind worn open in sleet
By free-thinking offspring of Shelley,
Aggressive, and Left untenderly.

No medals, no citations, no codes
Of conclusions, by which all notions
Are infamous or accepted.

I do not decline that cress
May be pure and green on
Water running over red quartz,

That fine sand may be printed
Delicately by birds of the tide
Fringes, there a minute ago.

Light I ask for, not with excess
Of cold or heat, strong sufficiently
To reveal, to you and to me:

Element, congratulating,
Accentuating, of a perfection
Which we can think of only;

Or not think of, fatally—
Cold, tentative, in the fog
Wavering, and finding only

The semen of evil, the source
Of rejection, feeling of loss,
Obsessive mildew of

Being always indifferent. In light
With light shall we enshrine the word
Enough till it sparkles, meaning

Enough now of plenty, but far from enough
Of extending and of dividing.
Inside red Ayers Rock

Rock crystal signed what inside
Our acts and our bodies
We are. It was light stronger

For darkness around, and made pure
From parching excess of heat
In the open. I say

Light is a centre correcting
Angles to nimbi, and in them,
In them we live.

Papposilenus

I knew, deceased, an Irish baronet and writer
Who drove a punt hard through reeds to land,
Picked up the slight girl (yes he'd picked her up)
Who was his passenger, and said I am going to be
A satyr now, and gallop with you through the trees.
Balls, cried she, and wriggled free, and hacked
Him there. She did not know what satyrs actually were,
Having no Latin and no Greek, but adequate
Lower-middle education, so to speak.

Consequence of a Full Bladder

Kir, coffee, calva, so I woke
And dawn, as I. Babel wrote, then "drew
A streak along the far end of the earth".

I slept and woke: now rounded an elegant
Thunder-rose, a Zephyrine Drouin over this
End of the earth up high, up high.

I was awake for rain: bats at my end
Of the earth had wrinkled into cracks, swifts
Of August flew down low,

Down low some pink mist held
Our plain, thunder, silence, drops,
Drops on butt lids, then

Butting butting butting of the suddenly
Excessive absolute rain, and I exclaim how it
Darkened our, and I. Babel's, earth deeply again.

Trôo 1973

147

Items of a Night

Of the moon only a dull
Speck of orange I see now.
And in the course of these
Twelve words occurring
This speck of moon has gone
And a meteorite has
Straight downwards fallen.

I was with you two,
Below our gate we counted
Constellations. The moon
Was interfering. You're
Indoors, now. I lagged,
The moon's diminished, gone,
One meteorite, I say,

Has vertically fallen.
I turn. Car lights from under
Are patterning a play
Over our midnight cliffs.
Your lights are out. I think
Under these gleams and cliffs
By now you both are sleeping.

Sunshine will have you up
By eight tomorrow.
There will be dry wind
And heat. By midday will great
Melon leaves be drooping.
News will have come, this peace
May then be broken.

Or am I lying? Shall
I wake up before the morning
Much as I walk to bed, and both
Of you, uncertain, who am
Always to the low tide
And bared rocks of un-
Peacefulness so easily awoken?

The First Folio

I have, sir, the First Folio
Of your works, in facsimile at last
In a case, wrapped up in a parcel.

Which though a fortnight has elapsed
I have not opened yet. It is a very fine
March morning. I shall cut the tape, remove

Your works from their case
And open them I think today. But hesitate.
What shall I read first?

Shall it be your sunburnt sicklemen?
Your brightest angel that fell? Your
Sea of this world chafed on

The Kentish pibles? I am not young,
But certain events always
Are present: Shall it be therefore

On such a night as this? Or may my choice
Happen to be in a Quarto only? Your wand
Broken, you would advise me

Cynically to risk making a *sors Shakespeari-
ana* in your Shut Book? That, sir,
I resolutely do refuse.

Stormy Effects

Rain. We stood by a ford,
Were unsure under the hull of a storm
Which sheered up, which was lit
By wide sun, and then stiffer and stiffer

Drove the rain down. And we had to run
Uphill to her home by the track
Which had been a heated hard
Brown before. Now wet to herself,

To her skin, she stood in her door
And she saw that I saw through her
Sodden white shirt
To the forms of her shoulders and breasts

Of which her loose shirt had given
No more than a hint before. She laughed,
She stared at the rain, I
Stared at her in the door.

The Great Bridge

Eyes are raised to the great bridge only,
And when this great bridge came
The ancient village here was done for.
Speedily did the great bridge thieve its name.

Nobody now wonders at the chalk cliffs,
Sees the church or yellow castle on the bluff.
Eyes lift from long barges creeping under;
Barges, wide river, and the high bridge are enough.

Heroes of guidebooks lived here, heroine
Of the castle was that sad Scotch queen.
They are forgotten here, the great bridge
Being absolute hero of the scene.

It darkens: a grand bow of lessening
Studs of light hangs on the high air.
A barge of new cars moves under. Cars, cables,
Piers, swim of reflections, gently disappear.

Hypnotized by this abstraction high in air,
Whistler, Hiroshige, are the words some say.
For the lighted bow articulates: it is not Then,
But Now; which is the better way.

Le Bernica

(from the French of Leconte de Lisle)

Lost on the mountain side, between two high walls
Of rock, it is a savage nook of dream that few
Have visited since years began,
Too high for sounds of ocean on the coasts
Below, or—forget them here—the sounds of man.

Sated with honey, curled hornets sleep
Inside delicious bells which creepers
Hang in the still air.
A curtain of aloes guards access, and springs
From fissured rocks tinkle and echo here.

Dawn throws a rosy bandeau round the height
Above this closed paradise of scented green,
And round the peaks there rise and run
Fresh tourbillons of violet mist, when this deep
Incense-burner meets the sun.

And when white lava of cloudless noon pours
Down, it sends small flashes only through
The denseness of the trees, which pass
Like liquid diamonds from branch to branch, sowing
Specks of fire upon a night of grass.

Sometimes, ears pricked, eyes sharp, and neck
Up straight, and dew along its flanks,
A kid jumps nimbly from the trees,
And drinks, its four feet set upon a shaking stone,
From hollows crowded with green leaves.

Birds swarm round, birds flit, from tree to moss
Upon the rocks, from grass to flower.
Some wet their emerald breasts,
Some dry their plumage in the heated breeze, preen
With thin beaks, and whistle by their nests.

They sing and sing, in chorus suddenly, mix
Warbling with their calls of joy, along with laughing
Notes their love-complaining goes.
But still these harmonies with such gentleness float
That the untroubled air continues in repose.

Only my spirit penetrates, breaks into this delight,
Plunges into the happy beauty of this world, feels
Itself running water, light, flower, and bird.
It assumes your dress, O primal purity, and
Rests in deity without a word.

Gale in the Nesting Time, by an Avon Bridge

Being a bird, having so to navigate
This fisty gale in its
Third morning would no doubt be weakening,
If one was an old bird.

It would not surely be
Exhilarating for a young bird; now
Being when especially birds take
Lowest, most straight courses.

Secretively they go, glide,
To nests. Of weathers
For them worst are these Shakespearian
Winds of May and leaping

Willows, as in that eighteenth
Sonnet, I would say, pushing
The car, pattering
Vegetation on the bonnet.

Grace Acts of Ourselves

Of grace acts of ourselves, of e.g. temples if in
Ruins on red rock, and gods (the better ones)
If with good sense now deposed, carvings
In cliffs of Buddha, books of hours, cities (few
Of them); of states of mind; fictions—all fictions,
Yes—in which is
What we name our spirit;—of these grace acts
And not excluding graces of the natural which also
Are, and which suggest; having of all these
Consolatory things so little sensed, is it—
Come clean on this, my few, few friends,
Consoling that on dying soon our
Livingness depends?

After the Party

They have gone—empty our rooms are
Except of you and me; and we walk
Out, into the slight rain.

Yes, cut and level is the relentless
Grass, we imagine trees performing
A laying on of hands, we observe

Late spreading of the great catalpa's leaves,
Agree to parade a garden is sweet, arms around
Each other, after they have gone.

153

After a Dream

God knows how often I dream of you,
After these years and years.
Then again we are in harmony,
I am again on the edge of your mystery,
You again on the edge of me. Awake, then
I know how I need you, but then, O then
I know that I made you.
Fifty miles away from me,
It would be useless to see you.

That Fat Rose

I chucked that fat rose, it seemed scentless,
That I did not know the name of,
Next to me, on the black seat of the car.
Then drove away. I saw big drops
Spill from its close folds to
The black stuff of the car, and that
Surprised me. I did not realize
It had been picked after the heavy
Thunder shower. Before I was home
That cherry rose had dried, and I
Was surprised again, the scent of that
Fat rose now filled the car.
But given late that rose wasn't
Rose, it was by then no more
Than a flower, it was an object
Which I repeat had wetted the plastic
Black seat of the car.

Dreams of Old Men

Dreams of old men are their norm of being,
They stride, all of the day is theirs,
The colour of their flowers is brilliant,
And they dream of women.

Gatekirk After Years

Having fixed a dry stone for my backside
I relax on this slope, again I regard
The dale: how, far away, twenty-four
Arches cross it, from shadow to shadow,
How without sound a train of linked
Beetles traverses, and makes off
For Scotland. I delay, don't scramble
Down to what I have come for. Below me,
The tips of Scotch pines; rooted, still
Lower down, in the secret garden. If
I go down, though I find no orchids, no umbels
Of purple small primroses (since
It's October), two streams will join,
Enclosing a vee-shape of green. One stream
Will flow out of darkness under a bluntness
Of sloping rock, one will ease out through
Bits of a cave roof which dropped and broke
Aeons ago; will gather, widen, curve
With minimal falls, to the joining.
Midges will rise. The grey winter bed
Of scooped rock above will be clean.
For colour, a farmer's blue plastic
Sack from floods of the winter
Will be wedged into rocks. A globule
Will shine in a cupped leaf of grey-green
Lady's Mantle. The great mountain, too,
Will appear over trees, half clouded
Or for a moment free; both thrusting
And resting, and always, if I look
That way, surprising. And I am sure
That by all of this hidden garden, under
The dull floor of this dale, which I am
Seeing again, I shall be coolly unmoved,
Though I shall wish to be moved.

   Do I con myself if I explain that I did not
Come into it first with you,
When you were as well new found?

Blue it is overhead
As such a discarded blue sack, through air
Which is lucid and warm and should be
The agent of wonder. For me, this is late,
In a late month too; though I am not,
In the classic way, dejected.

     Yesterday, first seen, you showed me,
Beyond Kirkby Lonsdale churchyard, along
The quiet of the Lune, Ruskin's View.
Conned, or no, late or no, I say
That was different. That was part of the hidden
Garden of you, which you allow me at times
To enter; miserable and cold as you had been
In the sarcastic school of old lezzes
—You pointed it out to me—high
Over the flats of the Lune, under the fell.

Scent Inclusive

Shit and lilies, they say, are scented
by different strengths of the same chemicals combined
i.e. that which is dropped on drives by curvings dogs and
that which scents obstinately gardens

In June, and funerals, and appealed much
to epicene painters in velvet jackets of the Ideal
concerned with the Virgin's white virginity or the sexless
insemination of white virtue.

Shit being shit still and Madonna lilies still
being flowers which break along green lines it does
to me appear that some noses need much rubbing in this
only apparent contradiction

Or in this varying volatility of an
identical substance, there being shit in some
sweetness if not sweetness concealed at times in
some shits, in our accidental existence.

Call to a Colonel

Having just seen a clock
Which told our time in jerks
Outside an undertaker's shop
I rang a colonel up.

He said "I don't know who
The hell you are. I tell
You, no, I do not die.
I graff myself in lives that make

More lives. I am part
Of their permanent legacy. Goodbye."
That was his reply, colonels
Having selves easy to satisfy.

Rock, Sea Water, Fire, Air

Rock

Essential is rock: in its extrusions let it not be
Too soft and friable, so too slatternly. Also
Let it not be chalk. With that I am not at home.
Let it not be—as a rule—too hard, too rough,
Too resistant of hard frost. Granite (though not
Basalt) I refuse. For preference let it release
Water, admit roots, breed flowers.

Sea Water

The property of sea water is colour,
Let its blue become rather more blue
Than light blue. Then let it spread
Shallowly over light and extensive sand
Into selected bays,
Making it green, but with blue still as neighbour.

157

I speak of sea water
As not too cold anklet-water, not too cold
Thigh-water as well.
I speak of it also as that
On which reflections rarely may undistorted float
Before darkness puts colour out.

Fire

Is less common.
Muscles of bumble-bees generate heat on
Chilly days: fire is much
Enclosed. Fires I have made best
Aren't metaphors: they burn
Rubbish of gardens or of hedges
Till wet leaves
Explode, and released fed flames
Ripple up, at last.

Air

Filling legged or breasted or big belly clothes
On lines on Monday—that is one thing.
But air does not have to move horizontally, does not
  have
To go violent, have to turn into power.
Air may rise also vertically
Supporting—along escarpments—gliders, birds
On infinite freshness, on which they play.
Especially good, not
Heated, not carrying frost, such air is at the
Beginning of a special day.

People Divided, in a Spring Month

White oil drums for a barrier;
To close what gap
There is does a car's extraordinary
Carcase stand on end.

A sentry in surly green
Comes out shabbily,
Examines, lets through one who's not
Detestable, if not a friend.

Houses. Are walls, no roofs,
No doors, no windows. And no
Hens. And what blue on to low
Rock creams, beyond. And round

Confabulate grayly most
Old olive trees. And what star-flowering
Weeds possess this now not turned
Hard orange ground.

The Landscape Gardeners

Brutal shuddering machines, yellow, bite into given
  earth.
Only rich Whigs, commanding labour,
Once had earth shifted, making lakes, and said
—And it was true—"We are improving Nature."

Somewhere

Our picnic ought to be in the morning,
When the sun rises,
When there is dew on our picnic table,
When the shadows of me, and you,
And of our picnic table, stretch far

159

(Into what could be the glade of an Elsheimer
     fable)
And I draw your two breasts (if I am not
More coarse) on the wet of the car,
And the sun rises and it lights
The half-rhymes, and there is
No one about,
And there is more
And more new light, not hard yet,
Nothing left of a night.

Take out the dry chairs, drink our coffee.
There are no fears.

Dulled Son of Man

Dark son of man, his hunched shoulders lifting,
Through tinted fog of frost goes down to work.
Green is reduced, of trees, distance
Accepting him is vague, grass of pleasure each
Side is frizzled gray. I know him. Grit is to be
Spread, ditches will be cleared, kerbs laid.

No, he is not wise. He does not envy scattering
Birds or, particularly, those that fly
Into this swallowing fog in white and scarlet
Cars. Man—his parent—ploughed up farms
And bent himself. Roads, roads, near Exit 22,
Are son of man's concerns. More cars

Swim by. Wrapped is son of man in his black
Torn coat (with yellowed shoulders, that he may be seen)
And Work, Work (the observing Philosophers do not
Observe) has screwed him too and gigantized his now
Warmed, hidden, hardened beetroot hands; which must,
Dull, dulled son of man, be taken out, and hold, and pull.

The One-eyed Archangel in the Zoo

He dozes, pushed up against
The heavenward grille,
He comes to, he complains again
Of being ill,

Stretches, exhibiting his
Featherless middle,
Loosing now and then an arc
Of splendid piddle

On to the kids below, who laugh.
Then again he mopes,
And will not swing at all
Upon his shiny ropes.

He realized the muscles of his wings
Were getting flabby:
Couldn't he be tethered, for a change,
Inside the Abbey?

He would rise up to
The fan-vaulting there
And play to visitors, at stated
Times, the Trumpet Tune and Ayre.

He begged, Give me
A trump of gold.
The Commissioners refused, and said
The music rights were sold.

No jess would hold. In the Zoo, then,
Watch him raise a dry
Scaled lid and flash the diamond
Of his one remaining eye.

How his cage stinks! He'd dropped to Earth
To act the Heavenly Reaper,
Was caught, and how ashamed he is that
Man should be his keeper.

Television Tonight

A black fly is crawling. And as well across my screen
Are leaves—antique sense, antique
Word—falling. A girl

Walks up from the infinite point of perspective,
Closer; passes in the unending alley
What may be named the point

Of Most: of most emotion, most rejection, and
Most recollection; continues; leaves
Continue falling, the black

Fly continues diagonally crawling. Oh,
Abstractions, Figures, Closing, Soaring, Short-
Coming, Falling, Being Void, Being

Not Here—Abstractions, O as in my father's
Litany in the damp church have mercy, being
Us, and to us our whole time calling.

Not in Our Cold Street

Tendernesses of those dead now
Do we not meet
Along our cold Albion Street.

As well as in poems, paintings, or
Quadrangles they contrived,
I say in a cloud,

In some slope or a coombe,
In pillows of cress, so green,
With white flowers, on a ford,

In a fawn beach seen, I declare,
May their tendernesses survive,
Encountering us, who are alive.

Encounter with a Kentish Bird

This parrot travels in a car,
He likes the way its engine purrs.
And tight his feathers fit. Best
Seen are tail feathers of the acid green

Of February nettles, light-
Edged each one with yellow. But
Some under-feathers of his wings
Are blue. About his cage, his home,

It would be foolish to suppose he should
Be flying past huge fluttering
Butterfies across the vaulting
Of a solemn jungle. This

Bird of Amazonian descent hatched
Our four years ago upon an avicultural
Farm in Kent. English as
Me or you, like most of us inside

The identical cage of "socio-
Economic forces" he's more
Or less, I fear, content. Certainly
Like me he does not read

The Business News. Companionship
Is what this being needs, and gets.
So now he shows his blue,
Climbs by his beak,

And chuckles, clicks, and snaps,
Because his friend and driver, with us
From Sunday lunching in the country
House, across the field at last comes back.

Children of Children, Though

Going home, after years,
I was astounded to find
The great fir in which
Owls nested, dead.

I did recall the reeds
"Bending on the damp
Confines of the kingdoms
Of the air."

And children of children
I had known, laughed,
Laughed on the green
Garlick of white stars.

Obvious Disorder

This hot day in March, month
Of my birth, I do detest;
Living is, if not contradicted,
Not confirmed. There are no leaves
To reflect the sun unexpected,
Nothing yet is begun.
A grey scab covers the red wall border,
Tomorrow it may be snow,
Yesterday it was wind also.
I look through trees, which do not,
As they will do happily,
Conceal disorder.

No Need of Crying

"As if to weep over one's own grave"—
But would it be so contemptible,
And so ridiculous, to weep over your own
Grave; if you had a grave,

And were not ash, a little in scattering
Caught in niches of a yew, most
Having sunk to the numberless
Root-hairs of our lawn?

You would weep over your own grave
Not for you, but because living had
One less who was conscious of living,
And light had one less who was conscious

Of light, and objects and *Gestalten*
Of objects; one less devotee;
Because after–dying, in short,
Is no break of renewable day

(But fortunately, no aching
Rheumatism also of the perpetuity
Of night or of nothing). O
If you could over your

Own grave cry, living you would be,
Light's admirer you would be, still
For the moment should I have
No need of crying.

Privacies

What with cold clear days this year
The leaves are late
And birds, it seems to me, fidget
Around and have to wait.
Treading and accepting tread are privacies.
I recognize a half-song, I see coloured
Primaries and breast
Of newcomers fidgeting through the bare neighbourhood
Of their last season's nest.
Privacies are treading and accepting tread,
So too rounding for the frailty of the eggs,
With the pushed breast the feathers of a bed.

The Green Park

Wet. The deckchairs are still out.
Green leaves yellow the worn ground.
No holders of hands or assailed lone
Elderly walkers either are around.

It rains more. More watercolour leaves are
On the way down. Red lights, red
Danger in close ranks, even now perfect,
Are the late geraniums.

I could think, No, there are none happy
Or not happy and no biggest city around
Or one only in which for a reason unknown
There is no living; not a human sound.

Storm Coming in Wales

A cloud shoulders—it seems suddenly—up
Over this unsunned Welsh hill. It is the ovoid
Top which is to be seen most grandly and whitely. Full.

But I concern myself momently now more with the
    dense
Teasing blackness which is forming against this hill.
There is no sun, lightning must be soon. I try,

Try to see into this plum-toned great blackness, this
Opaqueness in dimensioned stillness. I smell the air. I
    see—
And you not here—pink as the pink lipstick you used
    some roses.

Nearly Extinct

Many warm creatures now
burn bright alone in worn-out phrases,
and their indifferent extinguishers
maintain themselves in cages.

166

On a New Oxford Anthology

Our new Edwardian interrupts his slumber
And stacks upon the flats of Humber
Photocopies of ridiculous lumber.

Ungrateful

"I'm not so often in the news.
They don't give me such long reviews,
I've licked the public arse
Since I was young
And now that arse prefers
Another tongue."

In Extremis

You know a Fleet Street trick or two,
You put death into all you do
And poets kill themselves for you,
        My Al.

First it was poor Mrs Hughes
You kept a long while in the news,
Selling her ovened in reviews,
        My Al.

Now Berryman's walked off his bridge,
Extinguished by the cold, poor midge,
And that keeps up your average,
        My Al.

And two to one on who is next
Beyond the remote Bermudas vext,
Since *in extremis* is your text,
        My Al.

But if another of your crew
Must drown in existential stew,
It could, it might, it may be you,
    My Al.

And that believe me, I'd regret
Because I keep you for a pet,
And do not want to lose you yet,
    My Al.

First Public Death of the New Year Season

Today we celebrate the death or rather
Mourn the concluded span of that
Little man
Whose say-so dropped the atom bombs;
By which began
As well the acts of Vietnam.

Of the two present Filths of Vietnam
One says "He was a giant of our times".
The other Filth of Vietnam
Says he led his nation with determination, so
Preparing his own grand
Strategies of filth in Vietnam.

At home our constitutional machine, our
Queen, cables we English always will
Remember this thin-lipped little man
And "his great personal and public qualities",
By which began
The bloody filth of Vietnam.

The Times, O god the Times, say a more complex
Man could never have decided to release
Those bombs upon Japan.
And I reflect that the mentally
Uncomplex ichneumon
Equivalently rhymes with Truman.

I mean that sneaking fly which comfortably lives
By making others die; as inconspicuous as
That little man
Whose simple thinking ran that all
The life of man
Must either cease or be American.

On If You Are

Digging the world or
Fixing on a star,
Everything depends
On if you are.

Possibly orgasms
Happen in the head,
You think of Pompadour, the footboy's
In her bed.

And going the whole way
In the funeral car
Living is the moments
When you are.

Dreaming, or clasping
In the bed,
Aliveness is
Before you're dead.

Poems 1975–1980

The High Castle

Set on their rondures rise,
Rise into the blue air, from most
Green slopes of grass, tapering
White paper towers. And never

In the well-shed turned now
Is the great wooden windlass
Of the most deep well. Here
Guides and parties only

Come and go. All now, all houses,
Are a depth below. And bridges,
Crossing a lake of river down
Below. Down, down there are

Lorries, affairs, vines, broccoli,
And flowers. And you two walk in
This unreal blue, on this unreal
Grass, circling the white towers.

Saumur

Driving through Dead Elms

Elms have died, over a green land
Is each, here, there, a leafless sad
Black upright drawing. It is
Winter in summer.

Through each delicate dead drawing
Sky shows. In some are black
Nests. But no rooks are in and out about
New life cawing

Before leaves are coming. Why must that
Which is all the time here, be now
Visible — the winter,
Winter in summer?

173

Visit from a Biographer

Someone I do not know today comes,
Dear Norman, from God knows where
In great America, to ask about your
Days in life. Today is grey,
A Sunday three weeks or so from yet one more,
One more Christmas Day. And it rains,
And a toad-house frowns, up our one
Road, a puzzled face. Squared eyes, a most
Red mouth. A facial fungus. With no neck,
And on the ground is it a parody of life.

This stranger: Am I to tell him where
You cut your name in the now
Fallen chalk? Am I to say
Whose silk stockings shared your top
Lefthand drawer? Steady the rain.
My newly washed white hair is wild.
A stir makes the gate creak.
Am I to say for whom, or why,
You wrote *Shepherdess,*
Show me now where I may sleep?

To Ivor Gurney

Wind-driven falling water flashed,
A blue passed, birds turned,
Wind made a growl and threshed.

It went through you, you flashed,
You were the blue, you turned,
You were the air,

Separate in a double-glazed
Kind cruel delusive false
Climate here. Your book

174

Of ecstasy I have picked up. It is
On my knee, at the moment it supports
My paper, and what I write, and me.

Hare and Burke

Maybe it is tragedy that possibilities of being
Fall short of exaltation of thinking
And exquisiteness and tenderness of feeling.
Still, the one is the condition of the others.

How I detest those antics of Hare,
His wagging cars, his fool's face and
His advancing teeth, capering above graves
As if there were no thinking, no feeling,

Only being; those antics also
Of Burke, black-chinned, sullen
In his open shirt, lurking in lecture-rooms
And in the dulled heads of the insecure,

Complaining that he is not loved,
Exhuming to denigrate and smear
Adipocere, and poison of his own personal
Chemicals, upon being; pontificating

On our times as if the phrase *Under*
The greenwood tree had not been devised
In despite of dying, in times of terror. As
Pasternak and Akhmatova understood.

Joan of Arc's Stone, Le Crotoy

Estuary without glory. Brown waters,
Plural waters, plural loops
Of more pallid intersecting selvages
Advance, hiss, and cover shine
Of mud and lap a fisherman's leaning

Black boat, surround it, and advance,
As brown as clouds. And clouds as brown
As advancing waters smudge
The supposed clemency of what we name
Heaven, in slow bars.

They wait, for the turn. Then cross
These flats with her — one or two
Birds lift — and set her rubicund
Chilled face to being
Judged, and fire.

★

Lay any flowers, sea lavender,
Mesembrianthemum, under the
Grey stone which tells you this.

Ones Divided from Evil

Homewards; having driven someone who came
To interview me back to the station. Poets, I now reflect,
As the sun Helios, Apollo, All-revealer by light,
Goes down in an autumn display of gilding, should

Refuse to be interviewed. They enunciate follies,
Slipshod. Then afterwards they think, naturally, of right
Things to have said. But I admit some questions of his
    now
Stir me to emotion. Helios has gone, and my

Emotion of man is that temples and gods were inside,
Through all our long time of unknowing; that as well
The best of our gods, and their temples,
For instance, that one in the brightest denying

Of storm or dismay on the top of Aegina, were better
Than a god might have expected, with reason,
Of his creators. Our measure is how much worse
Might have been our so imperfect unknowing creations.

Scent pinched from thyme. And always evil a Nixon
Or Childeric. Those evil who crash lids of their
Treasure on to evil hands of their children. And the scent
Of herbs and, after all correcting, of ones divided from
    evil.

Morning of Zero

Looking out of the window
Through the soul of man
I see Zero smoothing the whole world
With a white hand.
Light is also white at the back of the hills:
When the sun clears them
It will loosen the white hand,
Roofs will darken and will steam,
Grass will become green,
But it will not much warm the land.

First Visit, 10.15

She was infamous, for great
Lovers in her day.
How her *château* has now
Outside and inside as well
Become stained and grey.
On panels the delicate paint flakes away.

From April Fools' Day to
October we pay
To see her curtained curved
Corner bed in which
We may suppose they lay,
Looking as if we cared what the guide has to say.

But how all spirit of loving,
Or of living, has crumbled away.
How the crown of this old
Creature ahead of me shows
Bald through her grey.
Coins tinkle, we queue out into day.

There's a breeze: it is just
Sufficient to sway
Clematis flowers, white ones,
And pink ones, hanging from a slender
Iron arch in front of the grey,
And about these the guides have not a thing to say.

The Fiesta:
Homines Ludentes atque Precantes

Geranium men pull through a high
Village carts which are pink and red
With petals of geranium. Spokes,
Rims, hubs, men, are petalled with
Geranium. So this over-the-ocean
Village plays, by custom and by rule,
And candles elsewhere today are set
In hollows of cathedrals on their
Iron trays and women pray, not all
Because they are old or mad. Between
These flowers, these shawled women
Who pray, these twinkling lights,
Questions I ask again. Time
Have we taken out of pilgrimage,
Difference have we deep-frozen
Out of seasons, darkness we have
Diluted, and have darkened day; and it is
Clear to me that now I shall never
Walk dusty and burnt, by day
Noticing the yellow poppies and black
Cranesbill and flowers of dampness

As blue as day, at night led by
The Milky Way; shall never
At last in the soft rain enter
That granite shrine, of that saint
Whose presence ever in Spain
Is fiction certainly.

                   Once in Norfolk, home
Of my ancestors, pulling to one
Side, I let a procession go by, singing,
Self-consciously bearing a Good
Friday cross to what there is left, which
Is not much, since level with
The ground do lie those towers
Which with their golden glittering
Tops did pierce out to the sky,
Of the shrine of the Lady of Walsingham
About whch Erasmus was scornful.
Did I envy them? But then making
A god out of the non-entity of gods,
Recognizing necessity, and rejecting
As If, tell me, my being, now,
What shall I do? Or what shall maintain
My being? Give me an answer. Is
It enough, willing myself to play
By my rules, and to pray by
My ritual, that is to reiterate
Hope, since no *deus* descends
Ex machina? Enough to be called by
All shall be better, by *At last*
Shall none be exploited? And out
Of the indignity of a knowing and
Worried animal being beckoned
In that way?
              Well, that would be something.
Saints to be sure I admire, thinking
In deserts, burnt by salt upon
Rocks circled by whales, licked
Warm by otters, cherishing swallows
Returned, visited by dreamers, even

By the exceedingly bad; or made
Wonderful in glass which is
The colour of poppies and cornflowers
And sticks of angelica. But
Excuse me if I maintain there are
Saints not superior to the secular
Martyrs of hope, or shall I say
To St Morris, William, of
Doves upon blue and of the blown
Willows of Kelmscott. What vision,
What moment of happiness in the procession
Of moments is expressed by the carts
And men with geranium scented and
Petalled, on this mountain over clouds, over
An ocean?

Aphrodite
(from the Greek)

Queen of this beach, here by
    The swell of the sea
I have a house which is simple
    Yet pleasant to me.

I delight in this wide
    Terrible sea,
I delight in your prayers for
    Aid from me.

Give me my due, then a breeze
    Will flow fair from me,
And help you, in love,
    And over the sea.

Young Death

And now it is the longest night,
And I am awake thinking of him
In this St Lucy's night.

180

How no fine-fingured hand sleepily
Moves into the slack of his side.
How he wakes up

And their full bed is empty. How
It is not true. How — lorries begin —
After all, after all, no

Body shifts by him warmly
In their bed. No one is here
who can be comforted.

Reflections on a Bright Morning

You are dead. So again and again
I return to contemplate this abominable
Brevity of living. How is it so
Loving and exhilarating, so always

Eager a chieftain of living should be
Living no more? It isn't enough
To say, Your perceptions remain; it isn't
Enough to read them, alone, out loud,

And to love them, and to remember you.
Whose investigating presence, brilliant
By day, hovered on shivering extremest
Wings over the night flowers of perfume:

You are not living. There is no you
To whom it can be something
That we live in part by your perceiving,
And praise you. And there, speak

With what resignation we may,
Is the distress. Remain mornings, middays,
Evenings, nights, and men's most curious
Coruscations. But, you are not living.

To Hermes
(from the Greek)

Wayside Hermes, this share of a fine
   Bunch of grapes, this piece
Of lardy cake out of the oven, a black
   Fig, an olive soft on the gums,
These slicings of a round cheese, some
   Cretan corn, a heap of fine ground
Meal, then this concluding cup of wine
   I dedicate to you. Allow the
Cyprian, my goddess, to enjoy them too.
   And I will, I promise, offer
On the pebbly shore a white-
   Footed kid to the pair of you.

Was Yeats a Fascist?

For ever the wild heart sings,
For ever they argue and they act the fool,
For ever at Coole his wild swans rise
And beat their wings.

Neither Here nor There

This is what he told me on the phone
Of the old poet, very long single
Hairs curling out of his chin, missed
From the bar, in the interval of his

Upstairs poetry reading: he was found
In the Gents peeing into his pint of beer
And muttering How awful these lefties
Are. And his young lefty admirers

Felt they were seeing life,
And touching the peculiarities
Of art, and surrounded him, and with
Embarrassment hustled him away in a taxi.

Funeral

I dreamt you were dead and your grace
Now was gone for ever,
And I was not there to love you,
Nor was your lover.

I sent a cable to your handsome
Feckless old father.
I could not remember the name
Or address of your lover.

There was no sign around of
Your husband either. So in me
I buried you, in a corner, and there was
No other mourner.

The Mynah

Is it the duty of visitors to this
bird garden
to admire Beauty?

    Meeow wow-wow replies the Mynah
    inclining his head. Other birds
    in this rusty bird garden I
    neglect. I listen to him
    instead.

Is it the duty of visitors to this
bird garden
to admire Beauty?

    Macaws gallop raggedly
    overhead, their bellies are red,
    meeow wow-wow this sad ape-bird
    for the tenth time says. I
    attend to him instead.

Is it my duty in this unsacred
garden of birds
to admire Beauty?

This noodle wags flaps of yellow
at the back of his head,
and simulates a cat, then a poodle's
yap. And I like that, I
talk to him instead

And though we may suppose
it is a duty in a bird garden
to admire Beauty,

and though pinker than usual in the last
sun shrimp-pink flamingoes stand
on one pin leg, what I wait
for is an eleventh sad, mad
meeow wow-wow from that cocked head.

Silly bugger says the Mynah,
Silly bugger, instead.

Riptete ton Obolon

Outside I admire, its foot ringed
With stones, a great leaning old
Olive tree fluffed with the two-
Toned yellow cream of its flowers, then
I open as far as I can the shrivelled
Doors, south, north and west, three
Sets of doors, to entice light enough
To photo in colour St Francis,
In a faint fresco, with the birds. But
Not light enough moves the black bar,
And I notice over a box a scrawl
Which says *Riptete ton obolon*.
The word *obolon*, I reflect, has no ring
Of April. Louis's poem I remember

And the hard black varicose veins
Of Charon. *Riptete ton obolon.*
It rattles into the box. Outside
And below blue heights and blue hollows
Recur, and daintily from a stone
Fountain water trickles away
Under fig trees, passes the sloping
Olive, reaches a gnarled *Liquidambar*
Orientalis, aromatic feeder of larvae
Of elegant moths, then goes to ground
Among flowers. One flower protrudes
From a spathe a black prick like
The prick of a dog, and it stinks. Yet
How elegantly curved is this black prick
Of a dog; how splendidly disposed
Inside on the green spathe from which
It emerges, are also the spots of
Ultimate black — if you take my meaning
Regarding, and disregarding, the coin,
Such being the elegiac deliciousness
Of season and place, of sunlight, of trees
And of flowers, of this small church
Here by itself, and its faded frescoes
Inside, and of you shaping all this in delight.

West Window

Consolations were: Christ, Heaven,
Judgement, devils at the mouth
Of great Leviathan, glow of these
Through minds stained with the bright
Salts of cobalt, copper, iron. *And now —*
What now, whispers to himself upon
His knees the priest, *now time hurts me,*
Home walks away, and deserts me,
And everything is beast?

His Swans

Remote music of his swans, their long
Necks ahead of them, slow
Beating of their wings, in unison,
Traversing serene
Grey wide blended horizontals
Of endless sea and sky.

Their choral song: heard sadly, but not
Sad: they sing with solemnity, yet cheerfully,
Contentedly, though one by one
They die.
One by one his white birds
Falter, and fall, out of the sky.

The Return

Summering mild-voiced birds have gone away,
In locked gardens are now leaves no more
Than moved by a small secret shifting.
Edges behind are smudged blue-grey of

A changing season. Under cliffs, under
The promenade's wild wiry tamarisks slow
Machines do not each morning early comb
The smart beaches clear of oil. Now

Grey and obese snakes in these locked
Gardens have again taken to sleeping
By the unentered doors below the continuing
Morning Glory slightly swaying flowers.

For it is ten days since cars, heavy with
Brown young and strapped-on, last-minute
Packages, sneaked home to their far off
Neighbourhoods of flats and factories.

Seville

Strangers only come to this strange
City by the routes of air. Then skirt
Forked olive trees in red earth speedily,
Then ragged factories.

A great cathedral. Let it be, the canon said,
So big they'll think us mad. Gold
Leaf of the Indies glitters up
To vaults of gloom.

The Discoverer's great black catafalque,
On great black shoulders in this gloom.
God must be buried here, he cannot live
In this great gloom.

Great heat relents outside. *Murderers,*
Guardia Civilia, Assassins, declare
Half whitened words across a perfect wall,
Blood of a bull — and

All crush round — reddens a TV
Screen. Needles of crystal water rise, Becquer's
Three girls in crinolines of marble swoon
Around their tree,

Astarte's doves, white doves, from palms
Flow down. This is, round parks, the city
Of Peru. Through trees a thin black priest
Extrudes his holy hands.

Then clouded flowers of jalapa, when dark
Descends and dancing sounds, are white
And frilled with pink and are at
Midnight most perfumed.

Epitaph

They buried me without
A penny for my fare,
So how long do I have
To hang round here
On this dank gapped
Wharf under this
Mud-reflecting sky,
Watching the polluted
Stream go by?

Musician with Green Wings

In that mouchette, too much aloft for poles
To smash and tinkle down, — listen!
In that high window, in that mouchette,
In a dulled, dark, damp church,

His green wings fining to a point
Over his head, on a red ground, one
Angel music-maker, floating,
Making on his long instrument

Such music as would later grand
Teutons between ages draw from
The possibilities of sound. On that
Damp side, faded Ecclesia

Triumphs. On this, faded blind Synagogue
Bends her deject, defeated head.
Dreams. This saffron music-maker
Is playing dreams of the dead times.

Hellas

If I say I have come at last home
And here marble is warm
And these shrubs are pink by the
Coarser rocks and shake by the sea.

If I say I have come home
And here walls are whiter
Than paper and here at last I see
How red wine does apply to a sea.

If I say I have come back
To the starting and here
White high boats lay slow
Magnificent breasts on the sea —

I have to admit to me, like all
Other homes, this home-as-before
Cannot longer, and as well
Warmly, be home around me.

Golden Find of a Small Clay Figure

Would it be, Goddess of Loving, since
Your clay cooled, say five thousand plus
Or minus a few hundred years?

Then the god-maker fixed this bead of
New gold into your belly-hole and these two
Gold rings in your ears.

The Great Headland

Who croaks Decay for all?
Who offers the Dove?
In the cliff-egg life spins,
And does not fall.

Colonels and Judges

Under oil lamps of evensong
God lifted up his face
And proclaimed a twisted blessing
On the twisted human race.

He was their invention who
Have invented worse,
Letting colonels set commandoes
Round their crumbling church.

The congregation leaves,
Guns titter round the graves
And those who are not corpses
Now again are slaves.

But now observe the colonels
On a waterless isle,
Shirtless and unshaven
And awaiting trial.

And observe the judges
Who've turned their coats again
To uphold with anxious
Virtue laws of God and men.

A Love Letter

Eurydice,
    A short retrospective and also
Prospective love letter. I have been reading
A critic of the plastic arts and I decide that like
The works of Ed Moses of California you are
"An idiosyncratic composite of tissue,
Nylon, and rohplex", which — now wait
For it — "is delicately and seductively
Tactile". And I thought — now, why was that? —

190

Of the goddess well-oiled (don't misunderstand
Me) arriving (on the way she had
Noticed with satisfaction the coupling
Of cat-a-mountains) to bed with Anchises
In his shepherding hut on Mount Ida.
Believe me, what an idiosyncratic compound
He found her, most delicately, and seductively,
Tactile, as she encouraged him to unhook
Her golden adornments, from Asprey's. Had she
The quality also of "seeming tenuous while
Being substantial"? Of course. Like yourself,
Eurydice. And did Anchises exhibit a continuing
"Predilection for discreet, hesitant effects, for
A complexity of quiet incidents"? The hesitancy
Was not hers, the subtlety was hers entirely.
But having this subtlest and most able instructor
He learned quickly. And on herself no
"Desiccated texture was exposed, or painted
Out in a pale colour". Also "dextrous execution
Kept the activity close to the surface". But
Inside deeply, as well. "Seductive material
And subtle effects." But on a real and not
"An abstract environmental and kinetic field",
On which, when the kinetics were over, well-
Oiled Aphrodite turned over, though tender,
To sleep, within a few minutes actually (you
Know what I mean, Eurydice) snoring. O amore,
Amore. Though enclosed in a perfume which isn't
Exhaled at all by the works of Ed Moses.

Chaire.

On Not Learning Russian

Peculiar Alphabet, you lay, in
My dream, widely, letting me in,
Conferring on me your unfamiliar
Shapes, your sounds also,
For the sake of him.

But it is too late. I look
Through your great railings.
Your avenue. Leading in glitter
To your palaces of more brilliant
Yellow and blue.

I cannot pick the great lock.
Now, Cold Alphabet, snow falls.
Too late for me to begin,
Too late to attempt to come in,
Even for him.

Halving of a Pear

An item of best being is
Halving this pear and in its
Ivory seeing this black
Star of seeds.

Also pointing this black
Star in ivory out to you,
And you agreeing, is
An item of best being.

The Fisherman

"Natives of the place"
Continue to walk in hard
Hide shoes with pointed ends. Increased
In width by ten, what was the strolling track
Of goats, kids, women, children
And men, is black and hard.
Sunshine remains twelve hours per day
In which wide glare a distantly big
Factory shows in space cleared
Of fossiliferous scratching
Rocks and delicately curving
Wild magenta flowers.

More must be fed, a new
Slaughter-house occupies a limestone edge.
More blood than in days of
Sacrificing flows. More blood
Flows down; out, into sea of blue,
Crimsoning an arc.
A man who does not work today
Fishes in the crimsoned arc he holds
A white carnation in his lips
And sucks the stem.

Harsh the glare is from mid-morning
To mid-afternoon. The hooter goes,
But not for sleep. A good globe
Our Earth was
For living as we can.
Most that is wrong with our good
Globe was always man. I become with age,
The poet of wonder in his letter says, more
Charitable, and all the time the more
Contemptuous of man.

Find in Hupei

Two millennia, two thousand
And one hundred years ago, and rather more,
You died, Han Emperor's servant of the middle rank,
And they embalmed you.

Now they've found you, in red liquor, in
Your tomb. And all your joints move supply still, if
They are moved,
And still you are dead. Your servants wrote

Your name on a jade seal, and slipped it
In your mouth. They gave you sticks of ink and a reed
Pen, and real food too, dates, ginger in a bamboo box
And fish and pork. They gave you clothes as well.

But miniature and carved of wood
Your horses of the wind, low water-buffalo, and
Boats and chariots surrounding you.
Inside themselves your servants knew that dead

Was dead. You would not live again. Or speak that
Name. Perhaps. But no, but no. You would
Not live again. And are dead still, and I
Say still for you, for me, Poor man! Poor man!

Deity not Deified

He would have lived, if they had cut him clear
Of that rock, if they had uttered the word
Over him, then sledded him downhill there.

He would have lived if they had pulled him
Up with grass ropes, and set him to stare, from
Shadows of eyes, out to sea, on a platform here.

He would have lived, if they had ever come back,
Ever divided him from the placenta of that
Mindless scarf-catching summit high up there.

In the Ford

As if modes and times remained the same
For ever they are there, a posing
Couple of landscape painters *en plein
Air*, as if they were strong Pissarro

And another, in a river, on their stools,
Their easel legs as well in water,
Below a broken waterwheel, bandanas
Round their heads, painting green

Shades and shapes on rippling
Surfaces. Two amateurs. I would
Not wet my shoes to round their
Elbows and to see what these two

Make of moments of green shapes
And shades. But that was years ago.
Whenever now I pass that ford I slow
And expect to see them stuffed or

Statues there, fixed, intent,
For ever — handing each other borrowed
Eyes, repeating what those grand ones painted
Over and over again. Yet all the same —

Watching Bonelli's Eagles

Bonelli? Was he Zeus?
Of course the bird-book does not
answer and I continue watching
them, thinking that although

"birds of prey" is our phrase
for eagles, they will descend
to eat at times coleoptera
and carrion; in which

they resemble, I say, if not
Zeus, lord of the white
Olympos, certainly ourselves; yet,
like this, to observe a party

of these aviators slowly
and broadly planing above blunt
points of mountain in cool
light (which has not yet

come down to illuminate
the minute black trees), in-
scribing a part of their nature
and cutting without change

of speed into each other's
sunny trajectories,
is suggestive at least of
strength and of measure,

minus pomposity or conceit,
an empyrean example to other
powerful eaters of carrion,
gods, or presidents

of states, or presidents of
multi and again multi-
national corporations, such
as down here we have created.

Occasion in Westminster Abbey

Deckchairs, in the park,
Are empty. A few
Walk below their umbrellas
Under yellowing trees. Pelicans
By the lake crouch
Pallidly yellow, and wet.
It is, over London, grey.

Inside, now, in the Abbey everything rises
And levels. Gently the frilled boys
Are singing gentlest music by Haydn.
Quid prodest, quid prodest, O mortalis?

Microphones cannot bring to the last
Stalls of the choir of gold
The old actor's voice intoning
"In the prison of his days

Teach the free man how to praise."
And we are blessed now. And I
Am not one to say no to a blessing. And
Now it is over. We tread recognizing

Each other. We pass Dryden to your
Black stone, Rare One, and read on it
For ourselves your lines we scarcely
Could hear. Poets are talking.

One is off, he says, in the morning
To Prague, his manner eager, his hair
Needing a wash, his glasses half out
Of his pocket in a frayed case.

No rain now outside, now
In the park again. No rain.
Instead a blessed low interference
Of sunlight magicking grass
And the yellowing trees,
Rare One, for a while into
Heaven, so that I do not
Care to repeat *Quid prodest, quid*
    Prodest. O mortalis?

Remembering George Barnes, on the Anniversary of his Starting of the Third Programme

Not given to Scotch eggs and shandy in the pub
But crushing poppadums in your Oriental Club,
Or pacing between B.H. and Harley Street,
Upset, dear George, and sometimes indiscreet,
You showed yourself, whatever you were at,
Never the uncultivated cultural-democrat.
You would have preferred pursuing knowledge,
Presiding over the best-lawned Cambridge college —
A cynic? No. Maybe a compromiser,
By nurture, between the average and the wiser.

For that we had the lip to call you shallow,
Nicknaming you the Pillar of Marshmallow.
But then you saw a condition of the mind to come
Pillared on caryatids of chewing-gum,
And salved your admitted treason to the Word
In that fine Programme so rapidly given the bird.
Ear-counting colleagues jeered at Barnes's Folly
And your ridiculous elitist squandering of lolly
Better dispensed to purchase nastier names
And set up series of more babyish parlour games.
"George will hire the Greek Ambassador to read, in Greek,
All Aristophanes, in ninety-nine instalments, week by
    week."
Yet for a while evoking the easy sneer,
Fine words, fine notes were waved through the startled air,
For a while the bay-trees in the black tubs glistened,
And even the Muses sent for a radio and listened.

I Did Not Say Content

It's everywhere, and if we are
Its archaeologists and dig, stale
Excrement lies under
Excrement, and further down

Most ancient and compact
Dried excrement; and under that
Lies coprolite, so many thousand
Excremental years B.P., B.C.

Yet here and there, don't get me
Wrong, is sacrament,
Both new and then to all depths
Stratified; of hand which holds

The hand. I did not say,
Sacrament which is priesthood's
Excrement. So, be comforted.
Content I did not say.

Kazanluk

Ourselves surrounding with symbols of living
And of returning to living,

For aeons we have been turning unliving
Away, for aeons charading.

So our young queen, abandoned to living,
Comes to this funeral feasting.

She lays her soft hand on her consort's
Arm, which is discoloured and chilly,

And to him tread the straight girls who carry
Trays of Persephone's symbols,

And the cakes on his table are broken.
Close the tomb up. Those living

Have come out to light. Fit the cut
Stones, heap earth on the mound,

Lash the horses, lean forward. Drive faster
And faster the cars of this furious

Living — your scarves streaming airborne
Behind you — around and around

And around. More faintly
Shrill the thin gold
Trumpets under the ground.

It Does Not Clear

To be seen, no cliff. Fog only, in which,
A substance, thorn-bushes, on the surface,

Are black shapes. Beyond, above, on either
Side this fog which is not shifting, is

Not moved away. You'd like to see riders
Along the cliff-top, jackdaws

On the up-draught rising?
Comforting; a film excerpt of this ancient

World. You would have these riders of
Which century? Slow,

Not too far to see necks of their horses
Curving, so much sky, so linear

A progression. Cavalry? Hunters?
Killers? Well, simple enjoyers

Of being in the air and young,
Looking ahead, seeing down

Over trees, over an endlessness of
Hamlet-speckled fields.

Even then if there was no fog as there is
Now, would your clear line of riders

Pass; and leave a blank and so destroy your
Earliest wonder of the day.

Crow, Rat, and Toad

To the crow leave the rat,
Refuse your arm to the toad.
Know what you are at,
On the identical road.

Death of Cicero

Slaves, you set down Cicero's litter,
And Cicero stuck out his head,
And with one swish a lieutenant
Struck off his head.

Did you weep,
Slaves, when you saw
Cicero dead,
And that rolling head?

Conversation with a Clerical Father

At times I talk to my dead
Father, I talk to him
About inevitable passing.

  I say, You were young, and then
Your young wife died.
You then, I say, required
The consolation you
Had preached. Years went.
Older, old at last,
Your whiskers fluffed and white,
Your hair behind a greasy
Iron-grey fall, I ask,
Did you take to asking if
In this land of life,
Of things you had hoped
To do, you had managed
Any at all?

  I can't say a mild sun
Warmed you finally.
I see you in the bed
In which you made a love

I'd think which slightly
Puzzled you, reader, by
Calling, of St Paul.
It was the bed in which
Your single daughter
And your sons were born.
And no hand
With particular tenderness
Wiped your great brow,
There was no hand to hold
Your hand. Only your deep
Unconsciousness then filled
The room. No thoughts,
You could not think at all,
About that better land,
My God, *that land,* you had
Heralded to others
Dying in their bed.

　O I do recall
How your broad thumb
Pressed on a short
Fountain-pen whose black
From age had turned grey-
Green. With that shakily
You wrote your words
Of life to me when I
Became twenty-one.

★　★　★

Now, lovers, rearers of lovely
Children, yes, and priests,
Enjoy, there being no
Better land. The broad catalpa
Leaves turn brown,
Wrinkle, fall and clutter
The wet ground.

Watch, while you can,
The November rockets climb,
The fire-wheels turn,
The silver fountains
Lighting naked trees.
And if you like, in being
Thankful — though to whom? —
Sink to an old
Attitude upon your knees.

Biology of Grief

Can I beat myself now for that
Grief? Evergreens do know their
Fall of leaf. In the end griefs

Are complete. Griefs take at first
To hiding away in the cupboard
Where photos of you and me

Fade, I walking under a black
Head of hair, you sweetly breasted
And slim; where — you removed them —

Are stored no photos of her; where —
I turned them out too — are no
Photos of him. We are older. Have

Changed. He and she — and you
Can't remember his name — in
Feature and age stay the same.

Swallow Cave over the Sea

Swallows have lost eaves in which they trusted.
These swallows curve to their grand conch
Where for more centuries than are known
They have nested.

Shark-boats heave by, planes in a vee drone.
Indifferent, uninterrupted, happy, a thousand
Of them, these swallows weave their
Wild summer home.

The Swallows

On a clear wire above a hollow of the air
Sharply these fat young ones strain their wings.
They peck, they trim, they act full-grown,
Then are young ones, quivering, when a parent
Curves from that great hollow of the air
Delivering to them insects on the wing. These
Birds are not aware of time, age, storms, weakness,
Tiredness, which are their enemies. It is we
Who have made up tales of them, they
Live without fear,
Without remembering. And they trust
Less to the hard earth than to the great
Hollow of the air.

The Swallows Returning

An old swallow, weak for returning
Yet compelled to fly,
He joins the young. They are strong
And stretch and preen, and are

Chattering eagerly. Around
Are favoured alleys and valleys
Of the air between elm trees,
Ledges, their dipping

Surfaces, known premises. Now,
Do they all lift and fly,
For now it is time finally
To leave all these.

Return

To the sea always this path goes.
The land dips,
Steeply this path crooks
Pocked dribbling rocks,
Upright on which such succulent
Pennywort grows.
Lower, to the sea
Corkscrewing, lower, lower,
This path goes.

    Always to a free
Infinity, beyond
The cut for wagons, the water-
Fall, sand-sunk stream,
And cowries
The path goes.

          ★

Always from the sea, back,
Rounding rocks, under
Black bent roofs
Of thorn, over
Worn slab stiles below
Wild sycamores, back, back, back
This rough path climbs, into
At last on top
This gracious alley, raked,

    And precise, of limes.
Here's the white
Gate,
Gravel, and the short,
Fern-green
Superseded tower.

          ★

Obvious the gravestones,
The parked car. It's late.
Say what you mean, I interpret
This lonely creak of the gate.
By the quaint, O quaint shot
Smuggler's stone *Know what*
You are, I interpret
The urging of a yet visible one white
Not obsequious foreign flower.

Pure Red

Lifting my face, eyes shut,
   To a lifting sun,
I consider this morning is
   Elementally and well begun.

In front of my closed eyes
   A situation of pure red
Floats, flickered with genuine
   Gold, till I turn my head

And mottles of purple
   And dull blue intervene
Which re-colour themselves to
   Suffusions of a blotched green.

These are not pleasant, so
   I turn back my head
And regain that elementality
   Of a most pure red.

Mosaic at Torcello

God's not to blame for God.
   But hell is hell,
Though God's cable goes
   Wriggling down this

Glitter-wall with voltage
   From his high seat
To start the flame. For that
   Are we to blame.

For God as well. God, have you
   Stopped judging? Now,
Robes off, do you wear
   The pit-rescuer's stinking

Gear, to save those twisters
   In the flame, who
Will not, rightly, scream
   Out your name?

If You Had Elected to Stay

I write — but the letter never is posted — "As I
Dream of you, do you dream of me ever?" Awake, I now
Piece together one supple dream of you. Listen,
Your hairbrush is rasping your hair. Then the scent
Of your still night-dressed body passes, and then comes
   near
And I say "Oh, if you had elected to stay, had
Elected to stay" — liking that form of my words —
As if it were not all those twenty-three years
Gone by, as if it were yesterday. And as if there was not
A concluding null summer fog outside under which
On the dull concrete the sneaking and stopping small
Lizards are grey.

Bright Piece Out of a Dead Sea

i

A sea of dirt, made chemical, of grey
Small waves below which not many fishes
Play, which not a dolphin breaks.
And where it comes to shore frogmen of
Archaics tack a rope to her. Seventeen
Centuries she has passed in water-twilight
Here. Saints — that was our fathers'
Name for them — clapped when Greeks stole
Gold laces from her neck, then, I admit,
Not dragging her sweet backside over her
Stony temenos or bruising her sweet fixed
Smile, carried her to the edge with care
And pitched her from this highest cape
At last, into her sea then blue.

ii

Give her a black pedestal in the best
Museum room. Publish her postcard. Establish
White doves in a cote outside. A television
Eye will see if you begin to pencil
Your name with your girl's name across her
Formerly pink thigh. But observe: most
Days this dead museum is shut. Her white
Doves have become grey. The Graces do
Not attend. She cannot dance with them.
And now she has not a thing to say.

A White Dove

Bedclothes heaped up
Shaped the bare feet, the draped
Legs, draped thighs of a statue
In my room. She was

The state of being young, or not
Too old for expectation, then
Surprise. Missing were this
Statue's upper nakedness

And the famous
Glance of her eyes. I dressed, I watched this seated
Fragment of the white

Deity of regretted love. I thought,
Let there fly in, the window's
Open, and to her knees now
Flutter a white dove.

Thanks, after a Party

I reflect on the evening before being
Seventy on the pleasures of not
Having met some who have been,
I deduce, sycophantic suppressors.

And on the pleasure of having
In the past sat on the lawn
At the feet of some who have
Greatly deserved our love,

And on the pleasures of having
Experienced epiphanies, not of
Divinity, but of endowments and benisons
Which are for us all.

And if this spring I have stepped
At last up the foot-burnished
Hill of Athene, for that too
I am grateful. Even although

I could, to be sure, like Yeats,
Complain I am one who might
Have had, to begin with, more
Of the love of women, yet

Excited I have been and contented
And soothed by that
At last which came grandly
My way; though with my own

Power of return I have been
Less contented. I who sucked
Honey out of the anthered magenta
Flowers of the fuchsia, have

Seen with surprise today
Features of my long dead in
The gathered living, with pleasure
Observed on mouths which

Tonight will sleepily kiss, again
That strangely continuing
Sweetness which shall, with
Consciousness, grow into kindness.

Death of a Farmyard

Worn out were the buildings, I
Tell you. Worn out. Do you know how
Buldings wear out? Elm walls were
Worm-bored and warped. Rain

Through the gap. Hard stemmed
Wide weeds in the track. Door hinges
Rusted, dropped out. In the lew, strapped
War-wounded Jim wove ropes out of

Hay. Smell of old hay. High
Nettles. Elders. Staddles, no, did
Not keep out rats. String-
Tailed quick feet, rats nipped

Into sacks. And believe it or not,
Two geese were dead and were dry,
Sitting down white around hollow,
Alongside low sties collapsed.

Pulled away, I tell you, all
Pulled away. No yard, no broken
Hay. No Jim. A new house. A new day.
That muck. All pulled away.

Corner of Somehow

I doubt the good of it,
But no one prays,
And if I say that where,
Into this hanger,

This grey mead cuts,
Below nuttal trees and silver
Legs of ash, where
A green cress flows,

Is a corner which is
Holy, I must mean
It is — somehow — deeply
Apt to man. "Somehow",

I must say as well, was once
The god by another name.
"Somehow" was his unspoken
Name; and to him

In these days, I say
Again, and doubt
The good of this, now
No one, no one prays.

Craft Centre, in a Derelict Mill

Regarding a blue punt drawn in, stillness
Of a secretive river, sparseness of uneven
Grass half cut, white and blue petunias
Bending from dry pots along a river wall
And amateur arts inserted in the decay of this
Corn mill, and over all to their
Crests huge river trees under a viciously
Hot damp wind swayed whitely — regarding
This, it's old Pissarro, bearded, who does now
Recur to me, since that which I regard, if
He had seen it (this corn mill then lively
With wheel noises, waters, stones revolving
And white dust of flour), now reproduced
In colour catalogues, or hanging in some dollar-
Tax-avoidance gallery, or waiting, humbly,
At a grand auctioneer's, would arrest or
Would invent summer perfection
Of this scene, the old lyricist's strokes
Of paint absorbing tattiness of unhappy
Grass and all ungrace, again. Whereas
In this, uncomfortably, I see impermanence
Not able quietly to be at ease. Again.
    Beyond this thin dry grass with weeds
A white wall has been broken through,
Leaving jagg'd edges; a wide warehouse
Roof removed. Cars are parked there, visitors
Crunch new gravel back to them, clasping
Their wrapped August purchases.

    Also, Pissarro, I have beyond these cars
Lined up, these sad studios, seen, neglected,

212

Away, out of time active, from the crunched
Gravel — stared into it — a white-stone
Well-head here. Some slates have gone from
Its conical black roof. Down five feet
Dangle inside, over black water, in a green
Circle, long hartstongue ferns, in a cool. These
Grow. These cannot be disturbed by a wind.
These are beyond the reach of hands. Are real.
Painted by you.

The Man from Byzantium

It was all very well for that royal
English saint to be martyred, they say,
On this shrill Cotswold hill. These monks

Say he picked up his head. Unoriginal.
It was all very well to erect that
Minster over the grass where he fell,

Too narrow, too dark, and too tall.
And here rain also for ever fell; and
The man from Byzantium purchasing wool

Blew his fingers, thinking of eating
His oysters again on the Lampsakene
Shore and seeing the glitter of sun

Run over the gold-leaf screen. He would
Be again at the centre of men, not
Knowing who ruled in the Land of the

Painted or in Chung Kuo. Not
Foreseeing either the Crescent and Star,
Or Old Glory, or Hammer and Sickle,

Or that Byzantium centuries ahead
Should be only the thought of a poem
Written by passion, which saw, in a green

Land even wetter and rougher, revolving
Cycles of time; where the myths were
Halted at least for a while, or

Paused for a while by the grim edge
Of the whale-furrowed floods of — before
Long — an oil-sickened sea.

Extinction

Thinking of your extinction,
I fear my own.
You were rock,
I am a loose stone.

A stone falls
And is reduced to sand.
Yet rock, stone and
Sand are parts of the land.

Issa

Seven syllables —
Busy on them
Till they contained him,
And confessed
Nature at work
In the one moment
When
It seemed at rest.

Birth of Criticism

Larking down the alleys, riled,
Where they are cluttered and defiled
I met a little squalid child

Perusing poems upside down
With a slightly petulant frown
Inside the very squalid town.

Squalid Lamb, I dared to utter,
Native of this mental gutter,
Thrilling to tell marge from butter,

What's reduced you to this pass,
Who should be gambolling on the grass?
Piss off, the Lamb said, Kiss my arse.

I'm reading — — and — — — —
And other masters of cold gravy
And *Imagistes from Tyne to Tavy*,

And my glittering Ph.D.
Will very soon enable me
To climb the professorial tree

And promulgate in flat reviews
Exactly who's who with the Muse
Of Forces, Fields and Avenues.

I gave a teeny cautious cough,
Again the Lamb exclaimed Piss off,
Piss off, you rotten *Sonnen*-toff.

And pissing off I said God damn,
How quickly does the squalid Lamb
Become the bullying pert I Am.

New Literary Memoirs

My goodness, they're already starting to remember!
I thought they weren't three decades old, but now
They're fifty. Some are bald. Some launch bad breath
Across club luncheon tables, fixing labels,
Some teach. Some write bad lead reviews each week.
Some nest inside the littlest little magazines,
As ever. And only yesterday the whole platoon
Appeared (but not to me) so clever.
Now knowing publishers are paying them to say
How — once — they saw George Orwell sporting in the
    hay,
Or some sly poetaster's wife caught in death's family way.

Respite

Thinking of unhappiness and marriages
I sat on my unmade bed, looked out,
And with surprise, wind having calmed,
Saw Buddha's great face rounded
In our trees. And back came
The wind, and broke the leaves.

Kingdom Come

Old men are glum
Not — or not only —
At the approach
(To them) of what
We once called
Kingdom Come.
They're glum
Because they've learnt
At last, they think,
How that bad-breathed
Fly-eating mongol

Child of Man
The whole while
Shuffles round and
Sucks its thumb.
O Kingdom Come.

Sicut Omnes

I visit my abandoned caves, white dust lies
On what is infrequently disturbed;
On forgotten books and old unbalanced
Accounts. In cavern stables rotten harness
Hangs out of the rock-cut mangers, and I come across
Tools, and weapons, whose handles of hickory crumble
The moment I touch them. Elsewhere old-fashioned
Clothes hang among cobwebs. Also another
Chamber contains certain beauties asleep, to be woken
Never, and that is myself alongside them.
Returning to green light, coming out into sunlight
Or into rain, that is better, under twinkle or falling
Of leaves. Not thinking too much; if I can,
Continuing aware, in my shreds of being, under
Leaves twinkling or yellow and falling;
On the low terrace in the old terms saying,
Although you may not listen, ecstasy
And then as well peace be with you.

Autumnal Again

From that slight dell Echo was first
    The voice of elves.
Then, in that temenos, among the quinces
And the roses, it seemed we could
    Forget our selves;

217

Who are always exiled, never
    Permitted to return,
To invisibles advancing, watching
The latest stubbles of the reaped
    Time lazily burn.

Downland Thoughts about a Poetry Occasion

Now a grey sky does the whole world house
Have they floored part of the Poets' Corner
With your name; I hear, next to Browning's
Stone; which is a cold fame, Gerard;

Who maimed your own great self; and worse,
Whose self was maimed by supercilious
Thin priests by whom, from pulpits even,
Now you are proclaimed, and claimed;

Who set with cold indifference your name
On the cold stem of a wheel-cross,
In a foreign cemetery, in a list of
Sparrow-names, O rarest Gerard, who knew and who

Declared how, under this grey housing
Pressing down, does the great sun break
Through, and suddenly, as now,
Does all our cold wide earth enflame.

Fling Away

Fling away up Cazy Lane
For great delights,
The grunting pigs,
The speedy growth,
The robin's nest, a
Day-moon in the west.

Fling away up Cazy Lane
For the hedge-sparrow's
Egg of the sea, in a
Nest of hills
From the top
Of the beech tree.

Fling away up Cazy Lane
For the plastic
Adder's convict dress,
For the bared
Breasts on the cliffs
At night, for the great delights,

Fling away, fling away.

Plymouth Hoe

Small stiff steps between the begonias
And a scent of nets.

So knowing and scenting began for one
Small Child of Man.

And the black, black frown of the bearded
Matron looked down.

You will die in your nice warm bed if you play
Like that with yourself, she said.

First Declension, 1912

Via Latina, out on the giving
grass of June, under
flecked ermine
of high

chestnut trees: what
was the surrounding
language then,
syntactically queer,

not Latin,
not English,
and not Greek,
that I began to speak?

Uncommon Epiphany

Love, for which there were few useful rhymes,
And which came only at times,
We wrote of like priests writing of God.
Moonlight silvered a sea alley,
Rain sparkled into a valley,
Love should be there, we said was there,
And it was absent almost everywhere.

In the Lleyn

How these clouds in this young sky curl,
   These ferns in this hedge are new,
     These nettles are young,
        And smell like sweat of a girl.

How this is spring:
   How these nettles are not so kind
    That they do not sting.

A Trôo, Les Lilas

It is possibly a time to fear.
He is young, he plays a silver flute
Among the lilacs on the cliff
And she walks to him with the light
Shining in her long hair,
And it seems that consequence,
Negation, and condition, disappear,
That *and*, as well as *but* and *if*,
Has dissolved in the scented air,
And it is not a time to be
Cynical and jeer, though
It is possibly a time to fear.

Stripes

Stripes which go
From right to left
And left to right
Are the bright stripes
Of the clown.

On the lady
In the lead
Of life
The slender stripes
Go up and down.

Gone

Gone. And I slipped half asleep
Into the warmth she left.
And I slept longer and dreamt
In the warmth she left.

In a Dream

She is old. Someone as if she were young
Is loving her in a dream.
How she indulges him,
How her hand wanders over his arm,
And how surprised she would be to know
She is loving him in his dream.

Washing her Hair in this Garden

Green her shampoo container on that orange
Table. And rectangle-shadows are
Slewed into blackest diamonds.
Now look. How her water-black hair falls again
Into the white of the basin.

September. In sun the thermometer over
The roses manages forty. She is young in this
Garden, how she stands straight
And is slight, now round her high head
Twisting a towel,

In this garden. And last night, last night,
Almost to freezing it fell,
And we were afraid for a thousand
Invisible wide subtle-sweet-scented
Belle-de-Nuit flowers.

Retained

I love to live, I live to love —
Whose excellent motto, excellent
Line was that, *I love to live,*
I live to love, the absolute theme,
Extruded, a god's arm out of the ground,
From the last seconds of my dream?

Names of Love

In private names of affection
Abnormals are the norm.
Love's names take expectedly
The unexpected form.

The Swan of Avon, for instance,
When Anne his wife came in,
And nobody was near them,
First kissed her lily chin,

Then said "Good morrow, Rat Shit,"
And it didn't upset his wife,
Aware that such onomastics
Squared love and disgust of life.

Tourist Note

Omphalos of the Once-World.
Blue hives. Traffic of bees.
Snow. Black-haired
Correct Japanese.

Grey glances of
Low olive trees.
Red, white, blue
Shaking anemones.

Indigo in this
Prestigious hollow.
Your cliffs. Your ruins,
Once-Lord Apollo.

Four-Poster in the Museum

Little urns surmount this ceil. Flowers
Are these curtains stitched in silk.
Its corner pillars I call not ivory
But frozen milk.

Exquisite is this bed,
And those who loved in it
Are dead.

Aphrodite and the Greeks

Tired of indistinction of edges,
Rain and white sides of blown leaves
He thought, How she stepped under those
Pink cliffs ashore. How they welcomed her
Out of the foam of surges of blue, how
To its one egg the halcyon flew,
Skimming that blue. And he thought, They
No more than thought those happenings too.

Spice for the Undying

Flame of a flat clay lamp does not dispel
The night, through which outside some divine
Planet goes. Bleats and moans from the pen
Of to be murdered beasts. Tomorrow,
Garlanded, their white throats stretched
Upwards to the gods' sky, before mid-morning heat
These die. Smoke for the goddess, profit
For priests, meat for mine and me.
Upon the smoking stinking portion for
My goddess, of fat and flesh cut from the bone,
A handful of Sabaean incense will be thrown.

Oedipus

Malediction to all gods
Who have created crime:
I acted ignorant of my acts, was
Blinded by my long fingernails
Through no fault of mine.

The Veil

A veil of air of the fall, of yellowing
Not yet independent, not yet
Quite dead leaves;

Through which are visible impersonal
Concerns speeding this brilliant morning on
A blue main road.

It would be the same, if clumsier, slower,
If an old century's rough waggon swayed
After farting horses

On a pitted road; if antique lovers or swagged
Mercenaries passed here: an ameliorating, half-
Hiding, intensifying

Veil in the air. A fraud, this veil
In the air? Veils are what young girls
At their marriage wear.

This veil of air: of points of yellow,
Without shiver. In this soon to be agitated
Brilliant air.

Tourist Island

This is a Greek sea-nest of blue.
Now, in a chill wind, at dawn,
These beaches empty, tourists sleeping still,

Parasols quiver, on their sides,
Huge hawkmoths tethered in long
Lines to the sand.

Eastward, and very high, over this
Not so vinous choppy sea,
Black Anatolia is a frowning land.

Annotation

Wind from Egypt blows cold waves
Across slantwise these rocks and ribs.
He digs — this ragged boy with sagging
Goats to watch — a bag of corms.

Cyclamens shiver at sky-corners
Of these brown, below-ground
Hollow long-robbed
Pillared tombs. Two jokes. Great

Pyramids beyond this slapping, difficult
Sea, then here these hollow
Also empty bourgeois subterranean
Tombs. These dirty sandy rooms.

Flowers on Silk by a Feudal Oppressor

A pity — yet as well — this ineducable
Bullace tree breaking into exquisite

226

Flower has no chance to imitate or emulate
The spray of plum Hui-Tsung compelled

To open up, on silk, in snow
(His signature is written below),

Eight hundred and some eighty-six
Comfortless springs ago.

Crossed Swords on a Midland Map

Blood on corn marigolds
On this brown open field
Makes the bere, that's what they will
Say, give double the yield.

Three kites hopping on this
Marigold ground.
The living have gone south
For their man to be crowned.

Masses are for the royal.
Masses are for the rich.
Sled these remnants over
The marigolds to the ditch.

As old are the bones of the young.
Get them out of the way.
Teeth in their skulls will scratch you,
When you reach for the May.

Paper

They might be refugees,
These scraps of paper
A leonine wind
Drives up the road.

Down there, past
Yews, a scatter of bullets
Tears trees not yet
Leaved. Tanks lurch,

Clatter aslant
The road; turn. Why
Has this wind dropped?
This fury now

Ended, snap, as if
There's been some
Hitch, some radioed
Switch of plan?

In this unbelievable lull
These tattered,
Miserable papers
Huddle in the ditch.

Gatekirk

Knowing home was, knowing there is no going home,
Knowing there is no home;
Yet stroking this mottled, sometimes as now sun-heated,
By the water shaped and polished stone.
Stroking this stone.

Hardy's Plymouth

Revisiting your marble-paved sea-perfumed town
I find it, like the middle-class family of that
Girl you married, much run down.

I know, bombs fell; but years ago.
Bombs smashed the Regency façades
Which led you uphill to the Hoe,

Whereon later no aching comfort could be found
In pacing the daisied ground, in a drizzle
Vapouring as usual from the Sound.

Now out of irregular rubbly open spaces
Dirty concrete rises and replaces your town's
Stuccoed dignities and maritime graces,

And only in a neglected dead-end lane
I've seen, striped black or rose, a slab or two
Of your old marble glittering in the rain.

The other slabs are uniformly matt and grey
As if your town were now re-paved with all
The more aching recollections of your stay.

The Park

There are parks in whose long alleys you seem on your
own:
In this one a seal barks, a slow priest is walking alone,
Three white girls also in marble crinolines swoon.

Where the alleys meet white nannies push their white
prams to and fro:
It will be hot as murder soon, high time for them to go,
And feathers fall in snow from tops of palms on which
grubby white doves coo.

Back in the grand alley where you may not cross the
wires,
Discipline of straightness, under great trees, is anaesthetic
to desires,
And that same priest walks on, whispering prayers,

Till the gigantic cast-iron gate is exit to the town,
So the black priest disappears into the traffic sucking up
and down
And being all alone asserts its veritable iron tone.

Apotheosis

A figure from an upstairs window seen
In a narrow three-hundred-yards-away
Long space of blue, between
Morocco green high trees.

White, in this situation, walking
Slowly, on — so once it was called —
A lawn, between high trees. And this
White figure is? A curio? From that

Junk shop in the right street
Which sells indifferent prints of
The Floating World? Now meaning-
Less? Fake? It may be. Certainly

She goes; crossing slowly now the
Perspective blue. She disappears. Her antique
Lawn now is a space again of casuality.
Between the morocco green high trees.

At one time, glimpsing her, we would
Have worried queerly. We should have risked
No disrespect. We would have
Gone down on our knees.

Crossing the Beauce by Slow Train, after the Harvest

Shines through one window, from the declined
Sun, a band of ochre. Through the other one,
Into mauve, above this plain, rises this new
Full moon. Benign seems the composite light
From these two luminaries, the visible and
The now invisible one. Sober the green,
Sober the brown across the endless
Undetailed ground. Nothing is ugly in this
Quarter light. No silo, no new house, new barn.

Peace, Peace, falsely or no, evenly these
Extents say; such as painters have made,
Such as the raised hand of a priest
May, to his old ones, say at the end
Of evensong; and within minutes now will this
Quarter light, for us travellers creating
Colours still, be gone, leaving outside
A night of unnatural silver, cold and long.

Concert, in the High Church

The Stranger? Is not beast, not god,
Is not angel and not — or not entirely — man.
A man-value? So you say.
And Bach calls. A trumpet calls.

He is here. But the great Stranger will not
Be caged in any sanctuary,
Exclusively; or stay for long.
Up to shadow-vaults and the white ribs

The trumpet calls, through the nave
Calls, out to a full moon.
The unforward Stranger — where? Smart,
In the first row? At the back, shabby,

Perched on the font? Winged,
On a capital? — does not stay
For long. He has, in nights, clouds,
Daybreaks, sweet days,

In pictures, playhouses, in our gestures,
Liturgies, in scattered minds
To roam. But — caged, caged
Never; never staying for long.

In the Spring Garden

Grass purpled by fallen Judas flowers,
Lilacs, between yews, in flower,
A yellow watering-can;
And I have taken a child

To the train; and leaves shiver
When hit by the heavy drops of the rain.
The senses — no, the senses
Or some senses do not harden.

But what expectancy
Have I now, in the rain, now
In the white of the May
In this late spring garden?

His November

Pens on his mantelpiece throw
Shadows twice their length. Sun
Catches the china boy, string, cheque-book,
Car keys, aspirins,
And so one more ordained, ordinary
Late-life day begins.

He's up — from dreams devised
Of a muddle of old delights; finding
A nearer seat inside the library and as
A sweet result of this
Sharing a pillow with that girl
He never dared to kiss.

His late days project no fine
Materials for dreams ahead. That's sure.
And yet it's not too bad, he thinks, as long
As sense remains
Of this mere splendour sunlight creates in
Condensation on his window-panes.

Again Discard the Night

Soundless, no lightest shift of the air. Then,
Slanting this blue indistinctness some bird —
It seems black — drives down, and there is one large

White and I know green-throated flower which has
Opened on top of the fence, and not yet do the
Immense and that one white round trumpet

Flower disappear. Forms become firmer out
Of the blue. Then you call, the kettle gathers
And talks, and *Are you all right?* comes your

Usual cry, and my habit insists, without sound, *Reply,*
Be bright, wash, shave, dress, and this once,
Again discard the night.

Difficult Season

Hot mists malform the constellations, and smudge our
    swart
Border of sharp hills to grey,
And less huge are the black leaves, which do not slightly
    move,

The hot wind having — for a while — quite died away.
There's no profit, no promise at all in this end of the day.
And as if that were not enough, as if all day we'd not
    been feeling

Flies trampling on our skins and tightness of slight clothes,
You turn remote: it is as if in you some
Unidentified resentment now uprose,

Blotting our mutuality and our chances of repose,
Except in sleep; and that will not come easily tonight.
    Thunder
Will grumble up. Then, those vague sounds, which are
    the first of rain.

Cool it will be. For a while. Light, sneaking in, will not
Declaim a green lyric of the dawn; only, after the longed
  for rain,
A smudge of damp, and heat, and the sullen flies again.

Une Vie

Two miles or so between a village and a town
She — well, lived, if that's the term, inside
A fence, a vegetarian, nudist, brown,
Elegant in her volumes, indifferent as to style,
Without a hint of invitation in her smile.
It's true, a husband came, her body had a turn.
She let him in, and let him out to earn.
Then children, and she locked the gate.
Postmen, and meter-readers, had to wait.
Books, neighbours, concepts knocked as well —
There was no bell — but soon desisted.
She had a phone, her number was not listed.
Bushes enlarged to trees. Along her fence
Sweetest honeysuckles grew, at last so dense
They blocked a view. Only tourists, in high
Summer, now and then peered through,
And thought they glimpsed the children playing
Or heard their mother sing. Outside
Negroes and students rioted, threatened
Species died, and judges lied. Inside, where life
Was never lived, death never died.

August near the Beauce

Wind sways pink of Summer
Tamarisk against the blue.
Drowsy, after an indigestive night,
I point this out to you.
"Perhaps," I say, "in love, at Blois,

234

This was a sight
Which Wordsworth knew."
"Or Zola taking notes," you add,
"At Cloyes, having *La Terre* in view."
Dwelling on this I disregard
The wind-swayed pink of Summer
Tamarisk against the blue.

This General

This general was a vicar's son
In the bitter trade of over-
Kill, and many dead owed death
To his much underrated skill.

Retired he lived inside
This mill. He read
The lessons in his father's church
And he had heard his father preach

Thou shalt not kill.
And when he died at last
Artillery sounded a salute
For this as some say necessary brute.

Mesolithic Excavation

It is a most ordinary thing:
They have found the mother in her cowrie dress,
And with her, in her arms, her dead child laid
On a swan's wing.

After the Epilogue

How selfishly alive we act his death,
Through Act 4, Scene 4 of his play.
How in the famous Epilogue,
In our false fine clothes,

We butter him with praise,
And now, our giant codpieces and red
Wigs returned to store, in shabby
Jeans live out our normal days.

Encounter

A thin knighted one with a flat zipped briefcase
Arrived, and he spoke to a thin one
And they started. I, invisible, followed them.
They passed through doors which revolved respectfully.
And they crossed a foyer which was subservient.
And they climbed a staircase which was reverential.
And the thin one who was servile, shifted his servile tape-
                                        recorder
From his left hand to his right hand. Into the room
Of the Great Visitor still I followed them. I, the invisible
One, was to him visible, and fleshly, and he kissed me,
Full on the mouth, and turned to the visibles, and said,
"What is yours, gentlemen, a whisky sour, a campari?"

B to D

Birth — we don't go much for birth,
It is a lower case letter we give to birth.
Birth is around, we don't care much
For the sound. But

With bloody old Death it's another matter.
Note the upper case letter.
Still a person is Death,
More than an end of breath.

Death is somebody still. With aconites
Death comes up out of the ground.
Death, damn him, does not go away.
Death looks around.

Extinction

I am like you vis-à-vis
Extinction. I am not
Any kind of a hero.

I see petals of a touched, loved, green-centred white
Rose, the last one, before August, fall. I hear a dirty
Featureless great cloud mutter. But at least

There's no need for someone, someone, to come back
And announce now "After all, there is nowhere,
There's not a thing, there are no sweet

Warm days, no cause for coward of hero, there are no
Ridiculous everlasting degrees
Below zero."

Deceit and Verity

Out of the mist, hollow of profound
Mist below, to us, above, a bell.
Then sun strengthening, mist elevating,
We shall in a brief time see our river,
Whites of its eyes, among trees,
Reflecting mist; soon reflecting
Blue.

White doves, captive, in their familiar cage
In that river garden, will shift, yawn
To a scarlet gullet, lift their
Wings, and feel warm and coo,
And coo.

At last, he will say, we know
Who wrote the Pervigilium Veneris.
He'll quote Aristotle on order, having just
Reordered his river garden, Racine, La
Fontaine on doves and streams, as if
In sun after the mist, under Ronsard's
Spire, we are not caged
Too.

Couture

War Film

A barn — no, not a barn, a great room:
Empty, narrow, tall, alone, woods at the back:
In front open, to infinite fields.

Inside, as I say, nothing — except against the far
Smooth end wall a tall ladder, but not tall
Enough to reach in the ceil a faint

Trap-door. You and I — we're outside doubting
Whether to move on, or stay; sensing there is no
Way, none, for us two out of this war.

Then — A squad, carrying slung sub-
Machine guns, in an unfamiliar grey-blue,
Trudge forward from the infinite fields.

They are friends. But these say gutturally — stay
Or go? — before many low slit-eyed
Swift vehicles lurch to us, out of these fields.

December

Is it a mean meaning
That there is no meaning?

This brown cloud-cliff ends
And light escapes, and spreads
Goldleaf on this lower morning land
And so, once they would have
Said, and so . . .

So, all I can say, so,
For this while, this meaningless
Sense of ending ends.

After Our Fall

Man wasn't divided: division
    Succeeded, persists, and is true?
Spirit of Man other than good
    Malt whisky, will not do?

Indifference is our condition,
    Indifference in different clothings,
Which is interfered with, so fightings
    Ensue, then slow-dying loathings?

Could it be we've learnt, now, too
    Much to continue, to indulge hope?
We have tried Emperor, President, Man, God,
    Protestant, Archimandrite, and Pope?

Am I to answer with a gesture, a
    Defying stanza, saying, Yet all, all
Will go well for us, spilt yolks, out of
    Unconscious Eden, after our Fall?

The Acacia

Slightly it leans, from the vertical
Sways, and a breeze turns back under-
Sided-white waves, running waves of neat
Leaves. Above, a great cloud. Then, blue.

What I see is calling back these
Conscripts of death whom we walk with,
Are quiet with, to whom, not
Overheard, we dare to say "you",

As if leaves, waves, broccoli–cloud,
Noble blue, took in and gave
Back now always to us
How they were seen, how loved by — you.

History of Him

Development of Him. Determined,
Him's ancestors, Him's descendants, Him's relations,
Him's early, Him's declining phases.

Him's here, bracketed between Him's double
Dates. But where are the works of Him,
Which study of Him erases?

Fool's Mystery

Worried by the fool's mystery
Of our being here, and finding
No clue in history
She started on a fool's degree in mystery.

Whoever heard of an antique she-fool
Banging her bladder of air
Solemnly, like that, academically,
Year after year after year?

Breakfast at 8 a.m.

I recall the queerness of the cries when a boy was
   drowned,
But it is no good sitting here and calling this slow
River innocent, guilty, sly, or deceptive etcetera;
Or most ominously blackly profound

In the tunnel of those barbel willows where
That holidaying boy was drowned — though in their
   effect
Most soothing are those blown willows under which
That river-soaked boy was found.

Child

Mornings begin with again thoughts
Of her dying, and this mourning
With vapours of rain in long
Sunshine blown off the shingles.

It's as if today even her dying
Were living; threads, spider's threads,
Are lines of a wild green
In wonder over the windows.

A shift, and angles are altered:
Now these fine lines are not a wild
Green any longer. And it is that wild green
I say to myself, remember.

Years Ago

This old small lady with no
Hearing aid was young and leapt up streams.
Love materialized only in her dreams,
In which she did not stammer.
Fading blue eyes edged white
In a net of wrinkles are
Dying Morning Glories of an
End of summer.

Not in a Twinkling

If there are no secrets, in which
Quiver and crouch the explanations,
And if there are
No explanations, accepting
That sharp crystal fact now,
That crystalline fate now, is
Not being contented.

If we cease worrying the intricate
Nonsense of our fate,
If we relapse,
Knowing we shan't know the hero
Whom we knew, then in our relapse
Shall we in the worst mode of
Dulness be demented.

Haydn, in a Neo-Gothic Mansion of the National Trust

Rents were collected. Footmen
Crept. In rear quarters
Kitchen tweenies spun.
Small scullions were whipped.

Yes, starvings were grudged
For blisters of the summer
And strained winter backs. And now
In this late evening

Of sweet art, the great hall
Packed, will this wide playful
Mansion — Gothic windows
Lit, below this

Hunters' Moon, fair
Mists arising — be playing,
Yet, its true, its
True melodious part?

A Look Backward through Perfection

The half-moon has gone down. Black
Leaves interrupt constellations.
A huge moth is flying to the sweet
Scented Belle-de-Nuit flowers which
A light would show to be scarlet.

We have picnicked to-night by a sacred
River. On its black, fish, without noise,
Created widening and widening haloes, catching
The last yellow of day. Looking back,
How the earlier sun, having lost

All discomforting heat, at Le Fresne
Revealed red coats of riders, rippling
Of horses, up the avenue ceasless
Intricate moving of specks of colour. Then,
We slipped to the river.

The Templars' Church

Ermined green slopes of grandest chestnut trees
Hug this grey town which we frequent today,
Against blue May and gamboge fields of rape;
And friends of middle ages bear
Their ancient neighbour in. His widow
And unmarried daughters hung with crepe

Creep after them and him. The rollers squeak. Late
Entrants rattle a big latch. Sunlight looks in.
The enchasubled priest points icily. Then, then —
How shabby over him are the grey stones of this worn
Templars' church — he intones again that momentarily
Deceiving chant which short-viewed men

Compounded of hope and rhythm for relief. Outside
Nightingale-hedges of small fields for miles are
New-leaf-green. Living — that's the habit still of this
   once wife
This priest, and us. He's done his holiest, he's covered
His gold cup. So I slip out. I look for the day's
Paper which forecasts to-morrow's life.

St-Neuvy-le-Sepulchre

St-Benoit-sur-Loire

Now that soft bubbling smoke does rise and rise,
That ancient scent down the nave
Drives, and the chill of these grand stones
I feel in my thighs.

May Day, Sunday — more, more
I need than this old heady perfume
In lieu of the gods, watching its bubbling soft
Grey clouds in the far pale apse rise.

The Spider

The lean spider Why
From his tunnel-web
In the crack darts out,
And there is no reply.

Sunbathing after the Rain

Lids down: and sparks of fool's gold constellate in the
   red;
And these spread; and yellow, yellow surrounds a small
Sun of red. I knuckle my eyes, till blood
Turns a Last Day's sun, in a grimness of purple instead.
I say then, in this ruffle of wind, Open, reopen
Your eyes to the brief chicory blue overhead.

Sight not so Good

Blurring eyes in age
Make curled wet
Leaves resemble shit.
To hell with it.

Though I do see,
If I could see,
How the reverse
Would be much worse.

Critique

To be praised by Creeley, Dorn,
Or Calvin Bedient in the *New
York Times Book Review*

May yet happen — no, not to you.
"At once epistemological and human
These poems confirm the view" —

That no balls are left
Unbounced at all
In a *New York Times* book review.

Addled Egg

Most don't know what "addled"
Indicates — so do we drop the word
Or form
A new relationship with egg?

O stink of water at the spa
Which portly Irish priests
Both drank and made,
Resembling addled egg!

For eggs (from hens) went
Addled, then they smelt. Shall we
For ridicule reserve
The addled egg?

We won't. The metaphor
Is dead. Today our egg
Occurs in paper oviform. The date
Is stamped. I do

Proclaim our modern
Egg is always good. And so
I beg, just now, enough,
Enough, enough of addled egg.

His Self-Disease

Scratching till he bleeds at fancy fleas
This writer suffers from a self-disease,
Supposing brightly
We must approve because he's sprightly.

To an Abusive and Ridiculous Art Historian

Plain contradiction will not hurt you.
Satire might, which is to speak
Of vice in terms reserved for virtue.
Luckily for you satire today
Moults in silence or has flown away.

Kennings

Moorland of blue
Glittering plain
Household of eels
Hall of the whales
Meadow of herrings
Shackle of islands
Necklace of earth
Handbag-mirror of planets
Merlon of hermits

Rummer of sewage
Quarrel of nations
Laundry of tampax
Highway of warheads
Cupboard of mines
Submarines' carrycot
Swayer of oilrigs
Coffin of atoms

Fishfingers' Carton

Bygones

The yoke no longer boweth the neck
 of the oxen. But beareth upright the
electric light in the restaurant.

The wheel of the jingle turneth no longer
 through the depth of the mud. But blocketh
 the gateway, ornamentally.

The cradle cradleth no longer, cosily,
 the baby. But is filled with
 geraniums in frilly pots.

The tree is no longer cut with labour
  into short fat logs. But
  th'electric fire, O god, simulateth logs.

The tap is turned. Mercifully the tap
  is turned. None windeth water longer —
  what expense of labour — from profoundest

Wells. But one hath jollily imitated
  the well-head with old tyres, and painted them
  red. And capped them with forget-me-nots.

Stately Home

*"Those comfortably padded lunatic asylums which
are known, euphemistically, as the stately homes
of England." — Virginia Woolf*

Patrons paid — and ill —
For poems, music, palaces,
Fountains, parterres and gods and nymphs,
From crops, rents, pigeon-house and mill.

We walk, for a fee, their alleys still.
Bees cruise their linden trees, arrows
Point tastefully to what was only theirs.
The car park is too full.

Pastoral pranks of Jacks with Lady Jill
Are told by beds, and Boucher's
Rosy hangings. On a green morocco
Table lies a golden quill.

Inside their chapel, locked behind a grille,
These first rogues continue condescending,
At ease, in Roman guise. And as before
We others foot the bill.

The O.D.

Must we reserve the Order of Demerit
For the horse-fly and the ferret?
Rather higher on my list
I place
The yanking moralist,
And then the rabid bitch and dog
Campaigning for the need to flog,
And every Kremlinologist.

Supplementary Obit

An old friend writes:

Goodbye to the ne plus ultra
Television dictator of culture,
Who was skinny and bald as a vulture.
If his taste in red wines was impeccable
His opinions on art
Were not worth a fart
And his mistress was not even neckable.

Reply, about the Advantages of Experience

You're right. Our elderly eyes,
If they remain alert,
Do the more easily recognize
Squirming in his primal dirt
Another verse-reviewing squirt.

Think Big

"Think big, think big,
Like us," scream
Inanity and Vanity
Marching to dance
A Belfast jig
On the grave
Of poor humanity.

Index of First Lines

251

252

253